DATE DUE

CHRISTIANITY IN THE ASIAN REVOLUTION

HARRY HAAS

Christianity in the Asian revolution

HELICON
BALTIMORE

FIRST PUBLISHED 1966
HELICON PRESS, INC.
1120 N. CALVERT STREET
BALTIMORE, MARYLAND 21202

Library of Congress Catalog Card Number 66–24851

This book is set in 10 pt. Linotype Times

Made and printed in Great Britain by
William Clowes and Sons, Limited, London and Beccles

Contents

Foreword

It would be possible to devise a route for a journey through Asia for two different people interested in the position of Christianity in that continent, which would lead each of them to the same places in the same countries, but would bring them back to the West with almost completely different findings and opinions. One route would lead the visitor from one Christian institution to the other, bring him into contact with Christian leaders, clergy as well as lay people, and give him full opportunity to assess the positive sides of mission work as well as the activities of the so-called "young churches" in Asia. The other route, which would follow the same itinerary, would include contact with some of the same institutions and people, but would open the doors of many Christian and non-Christians free from such institutional bonds —though these Christians would, of course, be loyal Christians.

The findings of the second traveller would—to a large extent—coincide with the content of the following pages. The first traveller would probably not agree fully with what I say, and even if he did not object to my main trend, he might be tempted to challenge a number of statements. My book has been written, in the first place, for that first traveller, and for the people whom he would certainly have visited. From my own experience I know how much involved Christianity in Asia is in itself. This can lead to blindness. Some people speak of certain situations of a fool's paradise. This is a harsh judgement, but I heard it from a number of Asian Christians. One thing is certain: events which take place in countries like China, Ceylon, and Vietnam, do not seem to have any impact on the attitude and thinking of Christian groups in neighbouring countries. There is a tremendous lack of horizontal communication. There is an even greater lack of evaluation and assessment. My contribution towards remedying this lack is this analysis of the position of Christianity in present-day Asia.

My contact with Asia dates from late 1951. In those days I was asked to assume pastoral responsibility for Catholic Indonesian students in the Netherlands. From that year until 1958 I worked with Asian students, first in the Netherlands and then in Germany. This involved me in the struggle of hundreds of young Asians, Christians and non-Christians, who prepare themselves consciously for a very difficult task. The Catholic Indonesian student group of which I was chaplain in those days claims to have educated me in Asian affairs. They and I were given a good chance, as I was of the same age as most of them. Even at that time we sometimes found it difficult to communicate with Christian leaders, especially with clergy in Asia itself, although we were heartily supported by outstanding churchmen in our endeavour to prepare young graduates for Asia.

From 1958 until 1962 I served Bishop Edmund Pieris of Chilaw, Ceylon. That was in the days of

Bandaranaike. Fortunately my work was completely in the countryside, although I remained in permanent contact with life at the university and in the cities. Moreover, I was given the chance of travelling in Asia and to Europe a few times during that period. The great discovery forced on me at that time was my discovery of the Asian people, especially of the ordinary man in the countryside. My bishop had given me the task of building up a youth movement in his diocese. We started in the schools, and it is there that I learned what I have come to know about Christian education in Asia. I had the opportunity to check this experience with the situation in other countries during my journeys. The schools' crisis of 1960 provided another opportunity for profound analysis and reflection.

At the request of the International Movement of Catholic Students (*Pax Romana*) I took part, in 1963, in a survey which investigated Catholic student life in Asia. The report of this survey was published under the title *Christian Student Leadership for Asia* (Colombo 1964, 194 pages).

The first draft of this book dates from 1963. My Australian friends Neale and Deirdre Hunter helped me to revise the text and prepare a final version. But even then the manuscript was kept in the drawer— both mine and that of the publisher—till I came back from another short but very intensive journey to Asia during the August and September of 1965. Having gone through it carefully, I am convinced that much of what I have said should be known to Christians and non-Christians in Asia as well as in the West. Necessarily there is a certain amount of generalisation, but this at least has the great advantage that one does not get lost in details. If I have tried to be objective, I have tried to do so with a very subjective mind—I mean, with the mind of a convinced Christian who tries to live in his time.

Naturally, my own experience of Asian Christianity is primarily of Roman Catholic communities and institutions. I am, after all, a Catholic priest, and I have worked in Asia as such. But neither my experience nor my concern is limited to Catholic Christianity in Asia, and I hope that my Protestant readers will accept the ecumenical intent behind my usage of the words "Christian" and "Catholic". Obviously, wherever I refer to general Christian experience I use the word "Christian", and wherever I refer to exclusively or mainly Catholic experience I use the word "Catholic"; but in many cases where I know that what I have met as Catholic experience is in fact general Christian experience, I have used the word "Christian" without qualification.

I hope that my Asian friends will not mind that I have been outspoken. If I have been compelled to detect weaknesses in Asian Christianity, it is meant to fall back on Christians in the West who have been greatly responsible for those weaknesses.

November 1965   HARRY HAAS

1

The Asian
revolution

The aim of this study is to try and evaluate the role
of Christianity in the social upheavals taking place in
Asia today, and the particular ways in which Asian
Christians are meeting the challenge of the modern
world. We will, therefore, be concerned not so much
with countries like the Philippines or mainland China
—where Christianity is either dominant or insignificant—as with those countries where Christians,
although in a minority, have, because of (or perhaps
in spite of) their past connection with Western
imperialism, a certain influence on national development. Even so, owing to the enormous diversity included in the word "Asia", some generalisations will
be inevitable; we hope, nevertheless, that what we
have to say will apply to most of the countries east
of, and including, West Pakistan.

How is Asia changing? What features of modern
Asian life can truly be called "revolutionary"? Before attempting to answer such questions, it should
be made clear that the rather fashionable idea of
"decolonisation" does not provide us with a satisfac-
tory starting-point. True, most Asian countries are
passing through what can be termed a post-colonial

era, and, obviously, the effects of colonisation and imperialism have had a most important influence on their development. It would be misleading, however, to confuse colonisation with "Westernisation"—or whatever word one chooses to describe the spread of ideas and techniques, originally born and applied in Western countries, but now rapidly becoming the property and equipment of men all over the world. Although the two processes have generally gone hand in hand, one has only to consider the example of Japan—a country which was never colonised, yet has certainly become "Westernised" or modernised—to see that we are dealing here with two distinct phenomena.

Further evidence of the need to distinguish carefully in this respect is provided by the fact that the withdrawal of the colonial powers from Asia did not stop the impact of Western civilisation. In many cases, on the contrary, the achievement of independence by Asian countries has only increased the one-sidedness of their relationship with the West, and resulted in a more profound "invasion" of Asia by Western influences. It is well known, for example, that generations brought up under colonial or semi-colonial domination were so well integrated into the ways of their rulers that, even after independence, they continued to support systems and situations which they themselves had formerly condemned. It was these "Asian Europeans"—as they were sometimes called—who occupied the places left vacant by the retiring colonial administration. These men, although they may have played their part in the national independence movements, were hardly aware of the extent which they had adopted the

mentality of the foreigners. The result was that quite a few of them never stopped talking about the "good old colonial days", especially when they realised that the building of a new nation was not going to be achieved without many changes and considerable hardship.[1]

Once we accept, then, that it is not so much the more dramatic processes of colonisation and decolonisation that are causing revolutionary changes in Asia, but the continuous importation of ideas and methods from the West, we can begin to break down this influence into its most salient features. One of the first things that springs to mind is, of course, industrialisation, which is having just as revolutionary an effect on modern Asia as it has had on Europe since the late eighteenth century. The objection could be raised here that there were instances where the colonial powers were not keen to industrialise their colonies for fear of jeopardising their own national economy. Britain, for example, preferred to import raw cotton from India, rather than set up textile mills on the spot. In this way, goods manufactured at Manchester could be exported back to India and other profitable markets overseas. Nevertheless, such a process caused certain changes in the colonies because of the introduction, first of machinery and technical knowledge, needed for the efficient exploita-

[1] It is obvious that the immigration of educated people of the older generation to countries like England and Canada from India, Pakistan, and Ceylon is a result of their education in a different world which makes it difficult for them to adjust themselves to their uncertain situation.

tion of colonial primary industry, and secondly of manufactured products.

Two important side-effects of industrialisation should be mentioned briefly at this point. One is the economic system known as capitalism, which, by replacing the old traditions of barter and payment in kind with an international system of monetary exchange, not only revolutionised Asian economics, but also, once Asia entered the international market, opened up new perspectives to her inhabitants. The other is the vast improvement in methods of communication—particularly mass-communication —which has made it possible, at least in theory, for even the most remote areas in Asia to become aware of what is going on in the world. The result of these two factors can be seen in some of the Asian cities, where there is a greater variety of education, entertainment, business competition, and so on than in large sections of Europe. The fantastic growth of the film industry in India, Japan, and Hong Kong, for example, has no parallel in the West. Modern technology is breaking through the traditional patterns of Asian communication—and, more especially, of Asian education—at a rate that is little short of incredible. Despite the unevenness of the process, and the coexistence of very ancient and ultra-modern methods, the suddenness of the development fully deserves the epithet "revolutionary".

A natural result of improved communications is an increase in the political awareness of the people. All present-day political systems, whether dictatorial, semi-dictatorial, or democratic, make their appeal to —and, in the long run, depend on—the ordinary man and woman. Propaganda techniques, civic education campaigns, and training in political leadership are useful and necessary weapons in the struggle to make the man in the street conscious of his political importance. Yet they are weapons which can easily boomerang back on those who wield them. The political awareness of the Asian people is an explosive force. The student population in Korea, Japan, and Vietnam have proved this point already, by acting *en masse* to compel their governments to withdraw distasteful proposals, or modify unpleasant situations.

But even more important for modern Asia than this growing interest in political parties and what they stand for is the organisation of the working classes into powerful unions. Vast numbers are included in these organisations, which, with strong leadership, can do more than any other force in Asia to encourage the common people to mass action. Not many people who have lived through the first half of the twentieth century would be foolhardy enough to deny the immense potential for change that is contained in the idea of a well-organised trade-union movement.

Underlying all the changes we have mentioned so far is one which has perhaps had more effect than any other single feature of the modern world. This is the almost unbelievable increase in the world's population. At first sight, this might seem to have little to do with what we have called "Westernisation". Yet it has been caused largely by the increasingly assiduous use of modern standards of hygiene, and the consequent drop in infant mortality. Especially in Asia, many children who would formerly have died from undernourishment or disease, now have far

5

greater chances of survival. A chain-reaction has therefore begun which is rapidly over-populating Asia. If we stop to recall that more than half the Asian population is under sixteen years of age, it will be obvious to us that the population pyramid, resting on a very broad base of youth, will soon be as high as it is wide.

This population "explosion" raises far more problems than the basic problem of how to feed everyone. For one thing, it floods the Asian labour market with a continually increasing number of young workers for whom suitable work is seldom, if ever, available. Unemployment, and its less conspicuous but equally crucial concomitant, *under*employment, leads to frustration among the young, and a consequent conflict between the generations—the impoverished, but numerically strong and vigorous, younger generation challenging the well-fed, but numerically and mentally weaker, older generation to provide it with bearable living and working conditions. The older men, expecting the same obedience which they had shown their elders, can usually offer neither wise nor practical solutions. Even those who realise the urgency of the situation are tempted to adopt one of two attitudes: either they try to make the old system work, with some alterations; or they take refuge in revolutionary, but largely impractical, theories.

It is no exaggeration to say that if this rapid increase in the population of young people had been the only factor at work in modern Asian societies, this in itself would have been sufficient to overthrow the existing social systems. The pressure of their economic needs alone forces governments to implement schemes which, by their very nature, disrupt the traditional patterns. The young are the first to be affected by these projects. Every industrial centre in Asia is crowded with young workers who have "escaped" from their traditional social and economic environment, and who are therefore open to any suggestions for reforming the present situation. And even in the villages, young people have either seen or heard about modern technological advances, which convince them that a new age has begun. Not unnaturally, they are eager to play their part in it.

The repercussions of this increased importance of the young are felt right throughout society. Especially through the expanding school system, where the education provided is more often than not based on foreign models, new ideas are imported into Asian countries. The result is that the traditional way of life, closely interwoven with philosophy and religion, and static—sometimes even stagnant—for many centuries, is profoundly disrupted by the introduction of customs and attitudes from outside. The young are quick to copy new ways of behaviour, either directly from foreigners in their country, or indirectly through foreign films and literature. The older people do their best to slow the process down, but novelty is a powerful force, and the new ways often penetrate far below the superficial level. Marriage traditions, sexual behaviour, forms of entertainment—to name only a few things—are being affected in varying degrees by foreign influences, and these influences seldom fail to shock the conservative elements in society. Furthermore, it is a rapid process, starting in the cities and spreading from there to the towns, and even to the villages and outlying rural areas.

7

One of the most important features of Western civilisation being introduced into Asia is the elevation of the faculty of reason to a privileged position. The scientific, or objective, approach to human life—implying that what cannot be measured and classified, is somehow suspect, if not definitely unreal—is relatively new to Eastern cultures reared on Muslim faith, Buddhist morality, or Hindu spirituality, not to mention such an intensely social system as that developed by the Confucian scholars in China, or the intuitive animism of the tribes in India, Burma, and Indonesia. It remains to be seen just how deep an effect it will have; but there is no doubt that the young are already strongly attracted to the scientific viewpoint. Considering that the system of popular education is rapidly developing, and that the spread of scientific literature has only just begun, we must assume that the present trend could easily produce a genuine ideological revolution.

But whether this is so or not, there is an undeniable tendency in Asia towards secularisation. Where formerly life and religion were inextricably blended together, and the world seemed a primarily sacred environment, today the forces caused by all the radical changes taking place—the population explosion, industrialisation, science, and the rest—are more and more breaking down old religious concepts, and putting greater stress on the world as a temporal place that has to be developed by man if it is to support and nourish and fulfil the human race.

It was, of course, in the West that men first realised this need to develop the world's potential, and the initial reaction to the discovery was violently anti-religious. Now there are many signs that a balance will be reached, and that human progress will eventually be seen as a marriage of scientific and religious ideals. But Asia has already absorbed much of the early extremism. Many Asians who have studied in the West, or read a certain amount of Western literature, have been tempted to give up, first their traditional religious practices, and secondly their very beliefs. Others follow suit, and soon a situation is reached where a large body of people believe in "nothing". This creates what has been called a "spiritual vacuum". It is hard to say how deeply Asian society has been affected by this process, but the student world at least has been strongly influenced. More and more disciples of such thinkers as Dewey and Russell are openly abandoning their religious life. There are also indications that an increasing number of young people in schools and factories are breaking away from the old customs and beliefs.

On the other hand, there are signs that the major Asian religions are capable of a vigorous revival. The work of Western scholars has prompted Asians to re-examine their religous traditions in the light of modern knowledge, while the influence of the great spiritual figures that dominate Western history—that of Christ himself on the young Gandhi, for example —has opened up all sorts of possibilities for a religious renaissance. Colonisation provided a perfect incentive for such a revival, by giving religion a chance to ally itself with the struggle for independence, thus enabling it to emerge from its traditional introspection and self-satisfaction. Yet it would be a vast simplification—if not a case of wishful thinking —to imagine that the revitalisation of Asian religions is a purely political affair. The philosophical and spiritual vigour of Buddhism, for example, which has made itself felt even in the West, must be acknowledged as proof of a remarkable internal strength.

This regeneration, in the face of massive inertia and antagonism, has provoked some extremely interesting developments not unlike certain trends in modern Christianity. The whole relationship between clergy and laity, for instance, is beginning to be questioned, as also is the relative value of the temporal and spiritual realms, and the religious approach to the challenge of the modern world. The uncertainty of the Christian faithful themselves, scarcely able to keep up with the developments taking place in their denominations, is no more confusing than the changes that have to be made by those who belong to the old Asian religions. All over the world, people—and especially young people—are searching for ways to harmonise the discordant features of their religion with the new social, cultural, economic, and political conditions of their environment. Particularly in Asia, where the changes are more violent and sweeping, the problem of finding adequate solutions is of vital importance.

In the following chapters, we shall try and show the role Christianity has played so far in Asia, and the effect it could still have on the development of Eastern countries. It should be kept in mind that during these tumultuous times the ideology which seems to offer Asia most—by its high degree of organisation, its far-sightedness, and its well-developed philosophy—is, undeniably, Marxism. It makes its appeal most forcibly to the ordinary folk, the so-called "masses"—the workers and peasants, the poor and under-privileged.[1] And it is these very people who are being roused to an awareness of their importance by all the great changes that are going on in Asia today. Their awakening is often greeted in glowing terms. It is the end of ignorance, the dawn of freedom. It heralds the day when each man will be able to decide his own destiny. And so on. It would be very naïve, however, simply to sit back and wait for these emancipated millions to be educated as if by magic. On the contrary, the energy released in such a process is more like that of a volcano.

And when we look for the leaders who will guide this force, and channel it into the most useful directions—who, in a word, will *educate* their people, and thereby render the highest possible service to their fellow men—what do we find? We find a thin layer of educated leaders, some academically trained and some self-made, scattered through society in a way that clearly reflects the multiformity of modern Asian culture. The feudal lord, the rural patriarch, the labour leader, the politician, the military official, the landlord, the *nouveau riche*, the graduate, the native physician, the priest, the emancipated woman, the student leader—these occur, in various combinations, in groups and even in individuals, all over Asia. How can their talents be tapped? Many of them are middle-aged or old; many have hardly had time to absorb the foreign ideas that were current in their youth, and are bewildered by the accelerated rate of

[1] The leaders of these mass movements are the educated. The difference between the educated Marxist leaders and most other groups is that they are directed towards the people and try to train up leadership in, from, and for the people.

change; many cannot understand the young, who seem to be drifting into an uncertain future. Some courageously face up to the challenge, only to find that the revolutionary nature of the transformation they see about them perplexes them and convinces them of their helplessness.

Marxism has a most efficient system for training leaders. Through its leaders, it can penetrate into every layer of society. It is elastic enough to be able to adapt and change position according to the circumstances; it offers new hope, and concrete objectives. Moreover, it has already been successful in coping with typically Asian situations. It presents itself as modern, as ultra-modern. It is working for a better world, both now and in the future. Let us look at what Christianity, in its turn, is offering.

2

Christianity—
a catalyst

Many people think of Christianity as a comparative
newcomer to Asia. Yet this is not the case. The
"Thomas Christians" in the south of India claim that
their communities were founded by the apostle
Thomas himself. Be that as it may, their ancestors
certainly became Christians when Christianity was
a very young creed. In Ceylon the remains of a
Christian Syrian settlement have been found, and it
is well established that Nestorian bishops were living
in China long before the Portuguese and Spaniards
took their missionaries there some four hundred
years ago.

It is true, nevertheless, that the main impact of
Christianity in Asia dates from more recent times.
The first wave arrived at a time when the Catholic
kings of Europe were very conscious of their temporal
as well as their spiritual duties in this world, and
there is little doubt that the prestige of the Europeans
was a contributing factor in the mass conversions
that took place in St Francis Xavier's days. This is
not to minimise the achievements of the early missionaries, many of whom had to fight against bad
examples given by Christian soldiers and merchants,

and what they considered the evil done by their compatriots. Apart from a few exceptions, however—exceptions like Matteo Ricci in China and Roberto de Nobili in India, men who had a profound enough understanding of culture and of their faith to be able to free themselves from the parochialism of their contemporaries—most of the missionaries of this first period were staunch loyalists at heart, and inevitably appeared to the Asians as representatives of a foreign culture. This unfortunate indentification with Europe was aggravated by the fact that the theologians of the time were too engrossed in the church's European problems to make necessary, and even (to us) obvious, distinctions and clarifications, which would have given the missionaries a better idea of what constituted the essence of Christianity, and what was merely circumstantial and adaptable to different situations. If the missionaries themselves often found it difficult to tell the difference between what was Western and what was Christian, one can imagine how the Asians saw Christianity, especially those who looked at it from the outside.

Later missions to Asia, though less directly connected with affairs of state, had lost little of their sense of Western superiority, being, by that time, imbued with the philosophies of "progress" and imperialism.

The net result, then, of missionary endeavour in Asia was that Christianity was presented to the Asians—and accepted by them—in Western dress. (And at that a dress which had been often patched and altered in the past!) One has only to look at Christian architecture in Asia—and the way ideas are expressed in buildings is surely one of the most powerful and telling means of communication—to see that it made little attempt to change its Western styles. Until very recently, there were scarcely any churches in Asia of which one could say: "That is thoroughly Christian and thoroughly Oriental at one and the same time". Worse still—though perhaps this partly explains it—the imported styles were nearly all of the "neo-" or "mock" type which have blighted European architecture for so long. It is ironical to think that precisely behind these exotic and anachronistic façades a genuine cultural revolution has been taking place. For Christianity has definitely played a part in the introduction of new ways into Asia— partly in spite of, partly because of, this very reluctance to change. Let us see how.

Historically, the main way in which Christianity has influenced Asia is undoubtedly through education. Christian schools are still considered the best in Asia, and their success is largely due to the great importance attached to education by all Christian denominations. The reasons for this stress are more varied than they might seem, and the desire to proselytise is not the chief one among them. In the first place, there was obviously a tremendous need for education. Parents wanted their children to go to school, and governments were willing to lend their support. On the Christian side, there were a lot of foreigners in Asia who could best be employed as teachers; and one of the best ways of securing a respectable place for Christianity—especially in areas where there were few Christians—was by setting up schools, and showing that Christian moral values were beneficial to a young generation, a fact which parents quickly realised and appreciated. Last but not least, Christian charity has traditionally always been extended to children, and the education of children is considered a guarantee of their spiritual, physical, and moral welfare in later life.

The most obvious feature of the Christian education system in Asia is that it was inevitably Western. This does not mean it was merely a replica of some Western model. Attempts were made, even in remote villages, to adapt to local needs. But, by and large, the outlook and curricula of the schools remained basically European, so that wherever there was a Christian school there was also a channel for the introduction of Western ideas. The effects of such a situation, on the Asian population as a whole, and on Asian Christians in particular, were quite remarkable. Because the schools were thrown open to Christians and non-Christians alike (and in many cases the great majority of pupils at a Christian school are not Christians), a Western education was imparted to a large and varied section of the Asian people. And because the Christian schools, having been set up and supported by money from abroad, were in a position to offer a better education than could be had elsewhere, a large proportion of their pupils went on to become leaders in the various branches of society. This ability to produce leaders is probably the greatest single contribution that Christianity has made towards the development of the Asian nations.

What has been said about the schools is also true of the other institutions on which Christians in Asia have lavished so much care—the hospitals, orphanages, homes for the aged, and the like, as well as more technical organisations for the improvement of agriculture and the promotion of land reform, cooperatives, cottage industries, irrigation schemes, and industrial projects. These are so many more agents of change, introducing new methods and attitudes which inevitably disrupt the traditional social patterns. Whatever their nature, they are all characterised by a typically Western quality destined to play a large part in the future of Asia— that is, by a high degree of organisation. This is perhaps the next most important gift bestowed by the West on the East through the medium of Christianity.

But, putting the general effect of Christianity in Asia on one side for a moment, let us briefly examine its particular effect on Asian Christians. We would, after all, expect them to be the ones to benefit most from the introduction of Christianity, and to have a powerful influence on their environment. For they were among the first to use modern methods of organisation; right from the start, the founders of Christian communities encouraged their groups to be disciplined and well ordered, so that they would not have to depend on outside help, but be able to survive and even expand by their own efforts. Again, this does not mean they were imitations of Western models. On the contrary, some delightful blends of East and West were produced. Any missionary returning home after working in Asia, for example, soon begins to miss the fine family spirit of an Asian parish. The community, far from turning Asians into Europeans, usually has the effect of conferring on its members a certain social mobility, enabling them to keep a foot in both camps. Naturally, there are grave dangers involved in sitting on the fence between two cultures. One runs the risk of being despised by both, and getting caught in a world of "spiritual half-castes". On the other hand, such a position offers special advantages to prospective leaders, provided that they act as sincere intermediaries and show they are at home both as Asians and as Christians. The temptation, of course, is that communities of Christians will prefer, for various reasons which will be discussed later, to isolate themselves, and take refuge behind a wall of conceit or self-satisfaction.

The question of leadership is a crucial one for modern Asia. It is generally admitted that there is a tremendous need for dedicated people who are prepared to make sacrifices. So many schemes and projects fail for lack of sufficient driving force to inspire the participants to persevere in enterprises which demand a spirit of selflessness rarely called for in the so-called "developed" countries. But it is equally important that the leaders possess, not only tenacity and confidence, but also a profound knowledge of the old and the new, of the traditional and the modern, of what is Eastern and what is Western, so that they can simultaneously gauge both the vital character of their own people and the exact nature of outside influences, and thus have a good idea of what will happen when the two are combined. Christianity, which has managed, through a chance combination of historical circumstances, to be in a position to produce a relatively high proportion of Asian leaders, should at the same time be able to equip them with the humility and the spirit of service needed for firm and reliable leadership.

We have touched on a very subtle problem here. For to understand the full effect of Christianity on Asia, to penetrate further than its influence on

Asians in general, or Asian Christian groups in particular, we would have to unravel the mystery of what exactly, happens when an Asian becomes a Christian. In other words, what is the social effect of the baptism of an individual Asian? Certainly, some changes would be inevitable. For even if the Christianity that went to Asia had been completely free from Western trappings, it would still have required converts to give up some practices or beliefs which might have been part and parcel of the local traditional context for hundreds—even thousands— of years. This cannot help causing a certain degree of disintegration, because every religion possesses an internal cohesion, usually comprising an elaborate philosophy, well-established forms of worship, and ways of life. It is perfectly possible for an individual —or even an entire group—to be converted to Christianity in such a way that the change shows every sign of being a progression, a growth, towards maturity. But individuals, no less than groups, are never isolated from their environment, and the effect of breaking them from the complex web of human relationships can, besides disrupting the former social fabric, provoke in the newly converted such unfortunate qualities as aggressiveness, isolation, prejudice, alienation, and a tendency to discriminate.

The only way to avoid tensions and conflict between different religious groups— or at least to cut them to a minimum—is to promote a spirit of ecumenism. To achieve this, each religion would first have to carry out a searching self-examination, in order to discover which features of its doctrine and customs are essential, and which are merely local variations that belong really to its cultural environment. For every religion likes to identify itself with its traditional surroundings; ordinary people, in particular, appreciate the sense of security this gives them. And since very few people have had the chance to compare the different shapes their religion has taken on in the various parts of Asia and the world, they find it impossible to distinguish between the essence and the accidents of their faith. It is this parochialism and ignorance which blocks the avenues to mutual understanding and cooperation.

It is no use pretending that Christianity is any better off in this respect than the other religions. In some ways, it is at a disadvantage; for there has been so much classification and rigidification in Christianity, and particularly in Catholicism, since the Middle Ages and the subsequent emphasis on Thomistic philosophy, that one almost has the impression that theologians have tried to build a fence of words around the undefinable. This has had a disastrous effect in the East, from the time when the Jesuits of the school of Matteo Ricci were forbidden to let Chinese Christians venerate their ancestors, down to quite recent injunctions that every new church was to be built in Gothic or Romanesque style.

It would have been far more productive to look for the aspects of Christianity which, while belonging to its very nature, also offer particular advantages to Asia. Nowadays, people are beginning to realise that the development of the world so that every person can have his fair share of God's gifts, is one of the best and most obvious ways of obeying the commandment to love one's neighbour, which is itself— and Christ made this perfectly clear—equivalent to the basic Christian injunction: to love God. Asia, where the need for development is so patently obvious, should provide not only Christians but all men with an opportunity to cooperate in order to do the will of God. For Christians to play their part effectively, they must see that a watertight system of preconceived ideas can be an enormous handicap in a novel situation. Each challenge must be met as it arises, if Asia is to progress without losing more than she gains. Christianity, which unequivocally commits its members to improving the lot of man during his life on earth, must use its influential position in Asia and contribute wholeheartedly to the realisation of the changes that Asians want and need so urgently.

3

The Asian Christians

We have tried to suggest ways in which Christianity is able to contribute constructively to the revolutionary changes that are taking place in Asia. It should be immediately obvious that there is no such thing as a Christian "party line"—a fully worked-out system of social development more or less valid for any country in the world. Christianity is not primarily a social or political credo, and must not be confused with any particular pattern of society. Although Christians in the West have elaborated a body of social doctrine, the greatest thinkers have always stressed that it is not meant as a manifesto; it is simply the result of rational thought, a sense of justice and a genuine love of mankind, applied through centuries of Western history. This does not mean it can be bodily transported to another culture, and set up as the final answer to all social problems.

The best way, therefore, of gauging the real influence of Christianity in Asia is to study the behaviour of the Asian Christians themselves. It will soon be clear that they are by no means all revolutionaries, despite the fact that revolutionaries have undoubtedly—in proportion to their numbers—had a lot to do with changing the face of Asia.

Since education—as we have pointed out—has been the basis of the Christian impact in Asia, we would expect the most highly educated products of Christian schools to have played the largest part in their country's development. When we examine the history of Asian nations (and of former colonies, in particular) we find that our expectation is fulfilled—but only partially fulfilled. It is true, for example, that the Christian schools can be credited with turning out more than their share of leaders at a time when Asia was eager to modernise. The list of administrators, civil servants, professional men—doctors, lawyers, and so on—, top businessmen, and top men in agriculture and education, is impressive. Of course, they were not all Christians by any means. But due to their Christian education, with its insistence on discipline and moral instruction, they were usually reliable, and had little difficulty in acquiring responsible positions in society.

This small group is the pride of the missions; from it came many leaders of national independence movements and progressive reformers. Because of these men, and because of the general goodwill won by Christianity for having contributed so much to the causes of freedom and development, the Christian churches—though intimately connected with colonialism and imperialism in Asia—managed to pass through the period of decolonisation without foundering with their former protectors. Even more remarkable than this is the fact that, in some cases, national independence helped Christianity to dissociate itself from the West, and gave it a chance to become truly Asian. Much of the credit for this achievement must again go to former pupils of Christian schools—many of them non-Christians— whose social standing made them influential in refuting allegations of imperialist designs (and some- times far worse) made against Christianity by its enemies.

On the debit side, however, it cannot be claimed for this highly educated group that they are all dynamic people with original and creative minds, aware of their responsibilities in the harmonious development of new nations. Despite the constructive role played by a few of them, the great majority are conservative—paternalistic towards their employees, servants, and the so-called "masses", and cherishing the ideal of a leisured class which they inherited from their former colonial rulers. During the struggle for independence many of the Christians among them were actually accused of not being nationalists, or at least of not being directly committed to the nationalist cause. Although it would be fairly easy to show that they were not the only ones to shirk their responsibility in this respect, and that it was certainly no specifically Christian quality that made them withhold their allegiance, the charge is, never- theless, a grave one, because it is directed through them at the education system of which they were products. If it is true that Christian schools failed to imbue their best students with a firm sense of social justice, they cannot be said to have succeeded in imparting a truly and fully Christian education. Let us digress for a moment, and see what could have caused such a situation.

In the first place, most of the missionaries who

have gone to Asia in recent times were recruited from regions where the industrial revolution had not yet disrupted the rather tired tail-end of the feudal system, and injected a new social awareness into the comparatively static traditions of the Middle Ages.[1] In consequence, many went out with a kind of puritanical piety, convinced that the prime need was to save souls and fight the forces of evil (which they often identified with the religion and culture of the country they went to work in). Needless to say, they were hardly equipped to see these "pagan" societies from a realistic point of view, and usually had little idea of the social and economic problems of the people they came to help.

Secondly, even those who had undergone the influence of the industrial revolution in Europe lost none of their sense of superiority. On the contrary, Western technical achievements and imperialistic successes only reinforced it. As a result, they had to carry a double load of prestige: the prestige they were accustomed to among the faithful in their home country, and the prestige they expected—as representatives of the West—among the Asians. Under these circumstances it was perfectly possible for them to devote their whole lives to education without ever having a true insight into the Asian situation. There were men who did understand the cultural traditions of their hosts and who could see possible ways of future development; but the sad truth is that even societies and institutes which traditionally con-

[1] As far as Catholics are concerned, the missionary personnel were recruited from countries and areas like Ireland, the southern Netherlands, Flanders, and Brittany.

centrated on education and social welfare work followed, sooner or later the well-trodden paths, and very often lost touch with the progressive elements that were striving for reform.

A third factor could be mentioned here. Christian educational traditions in the West have been strongly influenced by clericalism. The very word "cleric" betrays this connection between the clergy and those who could write, the clerks. As a result, education has never quite freed itself from the monastery. These features were carried over to the Asian system, because the missionaries mostly came from areas with strong traditions of celibacy and monasticism. Naturally, this does not apply so much to Christian denominations which have abandoned such aspects of their religion, even to dispensing with the clergy altogether. But, even in these cases, similar attitudes to Asian society at large would seem to indicate that the old ways die hard. Obviously, in countries that are in the process of revolutionary social change, any tendency on the part of teachers and leaders to withdraw into a cloistered world of their own, or to persuade their pupils and followers of the advantages of an isolated spirituality, cannot be considered as a positive contribution to the nation's progress.

Lastly, another ideal which passed into Christian education systems in Asia was that of an "elite". This rather feudal concept implied that the schools did their best to produce a set of literate, responsible people who would take their place in society as perfect examples of the benefit of a Christian education. In practice, however, this elite was rarely dynamic. The idea was introduced at a time when Asia was more or less static, and—since they had originated in the more traditional parts of Europe in the first place—the result was that the missionaries were content if their pupils went on to become models of diligence and obedience in their particular field, without suspecting that Asia was about to enter a period of profound change and would therefore need men of far more foresight and imagination than the Christian schools were intent on turning out. Here again, some understood the situation better than others; but most saw Asia as a purely religious problem, and were simply not capable of assessing her social needs. Consequently there was general satisfaction about the Christian achievement in education, though in reality Christian education was inadequately geared to the societies which it served.

Now let us turn to the less fortunate products of Christian schools—those who have received a good general education, but have not managed to become members of this privileged elite. These are far more in number than the first group, since Christians, being nearly always in a minority in Asia, and often belonging to minor castes or small ethnic pockets, have seldom been welcome at the highest levels. The schools have produced more and more students who are suited only for office jobs, thus causing a glut of semi-qualified people—a kind of stereotyped "intellectual proletariat"—many of whom cannot get a job at all, much less the sort of job that their education has led them to expect. The energy of this class has never been tapped. Their dissatisfaction at not being able to rise to the wealth and leisure they feel they deserve makes them bitter. Despite their rather humdrum, *petit-bourgeois* lives, they are changeable and easily influenced. In fact, they tend distinctly to the

Left, especially if they are approached with propaganda that is pitched at their level and directed against the people in power. Well led, they could be a strong force for good; they are much more in contact with the workers and peasants than their wealthier rivals in the elite, and often take leading roles in trade unions, cooperative movements, community development schemes, and the like. At present, however, their insecurity prevents them from making much in the way of a positive contribution to progress.

A similar situation exists in the rural schools. These are usually only smaller editions of their urban counterparts, since the teachers that work in the countryside are trained no differently from those in the towns, and the pupils are equally hopeful that they will receive an education entitling them to work and keep their hands clean at the same time. Here again, a frustrated group of intelligent young people is produced, for whom there are never enough jobs in the area. As a result, the best pupils are encouraged to continue their studies elsewhere. Although this is by no means unusual, it draws away potential leaders from the rural environment, so that the locality gets little in return for its investment—except, perhaps, for a certain paternalistic protection and benevolence from those of its sons who manage to rise to influential positions, and happen not to lose a sense of loyalty towards their native soil. Thus much of the good that the Christian schools have achieved in the country—the enormous improvement in literacy among the rural population, for example, which is such an essential basis for further development—risks being left without effective guidance.

Another disturbing feature of rural schools (which are, after all, of crucial importance in a still largely agricultural Asia) is a noticeable underestimation of the role of the teachers. Schoolteachers in general, and village schoolteachers in particular, constitute a most influential class of social leaders. They are in touch both with their own locality and with events in the world at large. They are also directly responsible for the training of future leaders—and teachers, as teacher-training facilities do not exist in many rural areas. Add to this, too, the fact that they are open to influence themselves, for representatives of reform movements and political parties know they can usually get a hearing from the local schoolteacher.

Because of their importance as intermediaries in the social system, it would be very unfortunate if teachers in country areas were misunderstood or in any way exploited by school administrations. Yet this is happening; a rift is already evident in many countries.[1] The reasons are not hard to find. Christian schools are very keen to maintain the high academic standards that have made them famous. In order to do this, and to keep up the traditional emphasis on religious education for the Christians, and discipline

---

[1] During the struggle over the schools in Ceylon in 1960, the great majority of Catholic teachers in the village schools worked actively in favour of the party of Mrs Bandaranaike, even after it had made nationalisation of the schools part of its programme in the second round of elections. The main reason for this attitude must be attributed to the tension between the Catholic teachers and the Catholic schools administration in most areas.

29

and a strict moral grounding for all, they expect their teachers—especially those who have been trained at their expense—to fit in with the old idea that a school staff should be completely dedicated to the school, and should consider its needs before their own. But the new generation of village teachers have wider horizons these days. They often consider their present job as a stepping-stone to better prospects in the future. The old system, where teachers were a part—sometimes almost a furnishing!—of the school, is rarely appreciated by modern teachers, whose loyalty is, quite naturally, divided. This split is bound to get worse unless the present attitude to school staffs is radically revised. Nothing will be solved by a superficial reorganisation of the administrative system, or any amount of reshuffling of the old pack of ideas. The answer to this problem—as to so many others, Christian and non-Christian, in Asia and the modern world—lies in a profound realisation of the responsibility of laymen in the development of what concerns them more than anyone else: the earth, and the fullness thereof.

Which brings us—having discussed the privileged and the average among Christians, as far as education is concerned—to the last and by far the largest group: the uneducated. Because Christianity has proved so popular with the illiterate sections of the Asian population, it has been accused of producing a crop of "rice-Christians"—a term which implies that people become converted only in order to benefit from the generosity of the missions, or otherwise to increase their living standards and prestige in the community. Such a morbid view of humanity is not borne out by the facts, and could only seriously be proposed by theorists with an axe to grind. The history of Christianity in Asia is not lacking in examples to prove the tenacity with which the "common man" sticks to his faith, even—as in Japan, under the persecutions of the great anti-Christian *daimyō*—in the face of torture and death.[1]

Nevertheless, the charge is not without an element of truth. In the past, the missions have spoon-fed the uneducated and underprivileged; and, though this was done with the best of motives, such a protective attitude smacks of mistrust. Now, however, everything is changing. The word "masses" can no longer be used as a vaguely pejorative generic term for the bulk of the population; it signifies not some great static, anonymous body, but a vast dynamic energy in the process of organising itself for mass action. The common people of Asia will not change as quickly, perhaps, as the educated classes; but the changes will be profound and extensive. One result will undoubtedly be an enormous increase in their freedom of choice, and a correspondingly wider range of responsibility. This alone will make the old, paternal approach of their leaders seem quite obsolete. The system of Christian community almost exclusively led and governed by the clergy will have to adapt, along with other religions and organisations, to the new circumstances. The present reaction among Christian leaders is often to take stern measures to maintain the old regime. They will have

[1] A fine example of this tenacity was the attitude of Catholics in Ceylon under the Dutch rule, when they were genuinely persecuted. They made a strong and bold stand notwithstanding the absence of priests, except for some Indian priests who worked in hiding.

to realise that the rousing of the urban and rural masses is a providential opportunity for the rousing of the Christian churches which have, until now, been working within very constricting limits. If Marxism has accepted the common folk at the centre of its system, surely Christianity, which is primarily directed to the underprivileged and unsophisticated, and which has so much more to give them, can do the same. The experience will be richly rewarding; not only will the poor be admitted more deeply into the mystery of their church, but the church itself will be able, through them, to achieve its full incarnation into Asia and the world.

4

The Christian community— leaven or glue?

Because Christianity is a religion of love, it must, by its very nature, aim to promote brotherhood. This community spirit is one of its most striking and attractive features. Community life, however, is by no means a Christian prerogative; it is a basic human requirement, which is elevated and perfected in Christ. In a Christian group, therefore, it is often extremely difficult to distinguish what is specifically Christian from what is generally applicable to human society. And it will always be difficult; for the more Christians commit themselves to fulfilling the commandment of love, the more they involve themselves in the extension of human brotherhood. For this reason, one is never quite sure whether Christians who are fully committed to any one type or level of social life should be congratulated or cautioned; for continual adjustments have to be made, if Christianity is to have its full effect. There is always the danger that a particular situation will be established as a model, and the principles and practice involved in its success imposed in other circumstances where they are not at all suitable.

Through their historical development, Christians in Asia are often found in ethnic and social groups which tend to become exclusive, or at least to pay excessive attention to maintaining the cohesion of their group life. This tendency to stick together and remain distinct from other groups does not arise from the nature of Christianity. It is caused more by the fact that converts often come from well-knit religious communities, which react unfavourably to what they consider a desertion. They see people give up not only the essentials of their former religion but even many of the local customs, to be replaced by new ones, and they naturally feel that Christianity is primarily a foreign religion. This was especially true during the colonial times, when Christianity was closely connected with the West. Since Asian cultures and religions had grown together over the centuries into complex knots of customs and beliefs, Asians found it hard to understand how a convert to Christianity could avoid becoming a Westerner. Were not all the missionaries from the West also? This reaction had the effect of cutting Christians off, so that they naturally tended to form their own groups and communities.

Another factor which fostered isolation was the fact that mission work was often undertaken in areas where conversion looked like coming fairly easily, or where the missionaries happened to find direct access to the people. There were instances when Christian groups emigrated under pressure of persecution or discrimination, or when they formed part of such groups.[1] Immigrants who had lost their links with their own religious environment found the missions actively at their service and accepted Christianity.[2] Remote tribes, too, presented a challenge to the heroic spirit in many a missionary; and social outcasts offered another obvious field for charitable apostolic work.[3] Sometimes Christian groups, established during a period of missionary expansion, found themselves without dynamic foreign leaders, and therefore allowed barriers to grow up around them for their own protection.[4] There were also groups created by schools, and almost entirely composed of educated people[5]; while others were just as exclusively rural.[6]

[1] This explains, for instance, why most of the Catholics in Cambodia and Laos are Vietnamese.

[2] This applies particularly to the Chinese immigrants in south-east Asia.

[3] The classic example of this is the mission work of St Francis Xavier and his successors among the fishermen on the Malabar coast. But another example, taken from the present day, is that of mission work among tribal peoples, and among the low-caste Pariahs in India.

[4] On the Malabar coast the Christian communities with a longstanding tradition of Christianity developed into closed communities, and for many centuries showed no actively apostolic spirit.

[5] In Japan the fact that there is a very high proportion of educated, and even highly educated, Christians, is a factor which hinders Christian entry into and work among the working class.

[6] One of the reasons for the present tensions among Catholic groups in South Vietnam—and, as a result of this, for the tensions between Catholics and Buddhists in that country—is the fact that the majority of refugees

None of these factors which have contributed to the isolation of Asian Christian groups is based on any essential Christian love of community, yet it is not hard to see how misunderstandings arose. Even more important is the fact that the distinctions between Christian and non-Christian groups have increased in recent times, in such a way that the Christians tend more and more to be a privileged group.

How has this come about? First, Christian schools, organised by the missions, have achieved higher-than-average standards of education. Although thrown open to all comers, in practice these schools have inevitably favoured Christians and prospective converts.[1] The same can be said of all the other charitable and social institutions catering to the needs of the people. These were continued and developed by specially trained native personnel; the family spirit being what it is in Asia, such organisations soon tended to become more and more introspective and close-knit, with an increasing emphasis on the institutional, rather than on the dynamic, aspects. This is contrary to the ideals of a Christian organisation, which is meant to have an effect on society like that of leaven on dough. Its influence should be not so much that of the groups as such, but of the individual

---

from North Vietnam are Catholics who were brought up in closed rural communities. These Catholics, and their clergy too, find great difficulty in leaving the ghetto which has given them security for several centuries.

[1] The proportion of Catholic students in most Asian countries is at least double, and sometimes more than double, the proportion in the population as a whole.

members of the group, acting on their own initiative, inspired and strengthened by all those who share in the community of faith. A certain amount of organisation is necessary; but it is the flux of human relationships which is ultimately important.

One more factor must be taken into account if we are to understand the isolationist tendencies of Asian Christian groups. In Europe, Christians have lived in a rather closed world for centuries. Before the New World was discovered, at the time when wars were being fought against the Muslims, who had cut Europe off from Asia and Africa, Christian civilisation reached a peak. It is this period that missionaries of recent times used to look back on with nostalgia. Afterwards, there were the heated controversies between the different Christian denominations, followed by further battles with rationalism and the new trends of thought which ushered in the modern age. All this has contributed to isolationism in the West—so much so that it seems to have become a typical feature of Western Christianity. This mentality inevitably passed to Asia, and played an important part in encouraging groups of Asian converts to keep to themselves.

Yet, one feels inclined to ask, if Christian schools were open to non-Christians—and in many cases to a majority of them—, is this not indicative of an open-minded attitude? And would it not counteract any tendency towards isolation? Doubtless, the authentic Christian spirit of brotherhood and service has never ceased to be an essential part of the characteristics found and encouraged in any Christian group that is at all worthy of the name. In practice, however, the presence of good qualities such as these does not minimise the absence of others—at least as important —to be specific, of humility and universality.

Of course, the way Christian schools in Asia have opened their doors to the non-Christian public is very much to their credit, and has contributed enormously to the genuine goodwill which Christianity has won in Asia. Nor was there any precedent for such a thing in the West, where Christian schools spent all their energy catering to the educational needs of the different Christian denominations. The rule of tolerance in most Christian schools in Asia is an unmistakable sign of the spirit of selfless dedication; and it is just this spirit which has inspired the incredible sacrifices needed to keep such an elaborate system going.

It is true, nevertheless, that the hospitality offered to non-Christian pupils in mission schools is of rather a one-sided nature. After all, these schools, though never set up solely as a means of proselytising, certainly have the propagation of the faith in mind. This in itself is fairly harmless for the non-Christians. They have a chance to live and work with Christians; if they are ready for such an encounter, the experience of meeting a philosophy different from their own, and of being able to compare and judge both sides, can be extremely rewarding. Those who do embrace Christianity usually do so sincerely, coming to it through a spiritual struggle culminating in a personal decision.

What shows up the unevenness of the system is the attitude of the Christian pupils themselves. Theirs is the official religion of the school; although the Christian atmosphere helps them to a better understanding of their faith, they naturally feel that their beliefs are strongly supported, and very often develop a sense of superiority. This is reinforced by the refusal—at least until recently—to discuss the relationship between Christianity and the non-Christian religions in any other way than that of traditional apologetics. The attitude of mutual appreciation, of direct confrontation and frank dialogue, which has recently been brought out by modern theologians, has not yet filtered through to the curricula of Christian schools in Asia. In other words, the Asian Christian population has so far missed out on a good opportunity to become prepared, in theory and in practice, for cooperation with non-Christians.

This is not to minimise the many friendly ties and personal relations that are established between Christians and non-Christians in these schools; this is surely one of the most tangible and valuable results of these schools, and its impact on society can hardly be overemphasised. It is clear, nonetheless, that the "equality" claimed to exist in the schools really means that Christian pupils enjoy a privileged position. This often causes them to do one of two things in their relations with non-Christians: they either adopt an attitude of condescension, or they keep their religion in a watertight compartment. Both these reactions are equally unreal. Briefly, then, we can say that, although the schools create an atmosphere of confidence and understanding, they do not equip their Christian pupils with enough knowledge or experience to enable them to coexist effectively with non-Christians. On the contrary, their privileged position only reinforces the tendency among Asian Christians towards isolation and self-sufficiency.

In the case of the other social and charitable

institutions run by the missions, the situation is made more complex by the fact that those who receive and benefit from the services are naturally in a weak position, and feel obliged to repay their benefactors with some kind of submissiveness. This is the eternal problem of how to help the underprivileged without crushing them under humiliating debts of gratitude.

In their present state, these services are certainly impressive. Most people agree on the importance of the Christian contribution to social and economic development, and this has become an established characteristic of Christianity in Asia. Much of the appreciation gained by Christians among all classes of society is due to their untiring energy in helping the poor and underprivileged. If they have concentrated on this work, it is certainly not by way of discrimination; it is rather a direct expression of the commandment to love one's neighbour. Yet, here again, Christians benefit most from the efforts of their coreligionists. To begin with, the social services receive a lot of aid from abroad; secondly, they are run in such a way that groups and individuals sometimes get technical or financial assistance which they might not have received had they not been Christians; thirdly, educated Christians often use their influence to procure good positions for their brothers in the faith. All these things mean that Christians are privileged. Some might prefer to call them better organised, having learnt the ropes after centuries of mission support. And it is true that they are relatively well organised, though not to the extent of forming pressure-groups. The age-old Asian policy of "back-door" arrangements is still good enough for most purposes.

On the other hand, Christians themselves are subjected to certain pressures. They are often seen as a minority that will not fit in with the general patterns of civilisation and longstanding religious traditions. Curiously enough, however, Christians are usually ahead of others in blending Eastern and Western ways. Their education has endowed them with a greater degree of social mobility and organisation than other groups, allowing them to make better use of modern facilities for development. This aspect is likely to receive a boost in the near future, owing to the increasing technical aid passing from Western to Eastern Christian organisations.

From the point of view of efficiency, this leading position of Christians in the social and economic development of Asian countries can be a great asset to the whole population. The services they provide are not restricted to Christians; usually, large areas profit from modern undertakings such as schools and community projects. And the fact that Christians are relatively more advanced in methods of organisation can act as an incentive for others to speed up their own rate of progress, especially if they have the offer of a generous helping hand. But Christian progress can also lead to too much emphasis being laid on group activity, in isolation from others who are working for the same ends. This means yet another obstacle in the way of mutual understanding between Christians and non-Christians. Especially in the case of a minority group under pressure from its environment, persecution-complexes sometimes develop, often brought on by the envy of the less privileged. Over-sensitivity to criticism is another unhealthy trait in the Christian organism, making it harder to suggest remedies.

Self-examination is the only safeguard against the dangers of isolation and privilege. Whatever happens, the present tendencies must not be allowed to continue. Nobody would deny that community life is essential for the preservation of the specifically Christian spirit, and for the mutual help demanded by brotherly love. This sort of community can make a very useful contribution to the highly diverse society at present under construction in Asia; but to do so most effectively, it must produce mature Christians, who feel personally responsible for the work of joining hands with people of other creeds wherever cooperation is feasible. If this happens, then the participation of Christians in the building of a new Asia will certainly have that leavening quality which is of the very essence of Christian life on earth.

5

The schools:
starting-point and
stumbling-block

Up to this point we have been speaking in fairly
general terms about the problems and potentialities
of Asian Christians. It is now worth while examining
certain aspects of the Christian influence on Asia in
more detail. The schools offer the most obvious
starting-point, not only because of the great importance attached to them by the Christians themselves,
but also because the Asian population explosion has
put a tremendous emphasis on the education of the
young. Most of what we will have to say is not
limited to Christian schools alone, but applies to a
general situation which is gradually coming to be
seen as inadequate in the present Asian context.

Perhaps the most pernicious fault in the school
education system being used in Asia is its lack of
contact with the environments in which it works. The
reason for this is plain: both in the country and in
the city, education is far too academic. Pupils are
trained to be "knowledgeable", to acquire "facts". But
very often this knowledge has nothing whatever to
do with the living context of the school, or the

human life that goes on outside the gates. And even when it does, it still tends to be pure rather than applied—with the result that a mentality is fostered in the pupils quite out of touch with reality.

This is precisely the opposite of what Asia needs. There is a huge demand for creative and imaginative leaders, for men and women who have had practical experience of Asian societies as they really are, who have run the gauntlet of modern Asian life with its strange, mixed atmosphere of hope and despair —people in love with action, who are not merely interested in, but also in contact with, the under-privileged. More particularly, people are needed who have acquired the necessary skill—the word "quali-fications" is not used here deliberately—to be able to educate others in their turn. From this point of view, the present system of school education is far too theoretical, and not nearly conscious enough of the community. That is to say, the schools are too self-centred, too keen to get good results, and too intent on turning out good, solid, and intelligent citizens who have little or no idea of their country's problems.

If any part of a child's education should make him aware of his responsibility to the world, it is surely his religious instruction. When we look at the Christian way of teaching religion we are appalled to find how little attempt has been made to adapt it to the Asian scene. The boys and girls in Christian schools are supposed to go out and give a shining example of Christianity in action; yet they are still being taught the catechism by rote. The language and cate-gories used are quite foreign. The underlying theo-logy is seldom expressed in suitably Asian ways.

None of the important questions raised by the meeting of Christianity and the major Asian religions has been considered, except by way of vastly oversimplified apologetics. The commandment of brotherly love is repeatedly put forward as a specifically Christian feature, without being translated—in theory or in practice—into Asian terms. Worse still, the training of people to be mature in their faith, to take their place as fully fledged members of a Christian community, and to make an original contribution to their society, has been very much neglected. On the other hand, docility and submissiveness are fostered to such a degree that most Christians develop a loyalty to their religious leaders which may be touching, but is of little use. As a result, any elements which threaten to disturb the status quo tend to be automatically ousted without examination of their merits. Communism, for example, is so thoroughly and dogmatically hated, that the question of social justice is obscured. The outcome of this kind of training is that the most active Christians rarely get the chance to become anything but an extension of the clergy. Instead of thinking things out for themselves and then putting their ideas into practice, they wear themselves out doing good works suggested by others, without ever really maturing spiritually.

So much for the Christian system; yet the same could be said for most of the others too. The general state of education in Asia is badly in need of reform. If anyone is going to lead the way, it should certainly be the Christians: their schools have better facilities than most, they have larger and more highly qualified staffs, and they are generally more coordinated in their methods of organisation. How could they use these advantages to help bring education into line with the needs of the people?

First of all, school councils and administrations must realise that they have no right to sacrifice their essential responsibilities to society for the sake of prestige. No one suggests for a moment that the academic standards, the high degree of discipline, and the various beneficial traditions that exist in Christian schools should be abandoned. On the contrary, they should be maintained and developed. But if they are allowed to set hard in a rigid pattern, or if they start to become aims in themselves, then they will inevitably be a burden to everyone concerned—to the administration itself, to the staff, and—most of all—to the pupils. There are so many minor features of school education—most of them brought about by the urge to compete with other schools, and thereby win "honour" and prestige—which drain an unreasonable amount of time and money that could well be used for other purposes.

One such purpose is a complete revision of the present attitude to the school's place in society. This is an essential preliminary to any overhaul of the education system. Teachers should be strongly encouraged to pay more attention to the social training of their pupils. Within the framework of the set syllabus, there are far more opportunities than are now exploited to acquaint the children with the human aspects of the subjects they are taught. If the school is genuinely permeated by Christian ideals of service and brotherhood, the education it provides will have to go a lot further than the mere attainment of good examination results; it will have to instil into the children a desire to pass on their knowledge and experience to others, and especially to the under-privileged in their own environment. It is obvious that this cannot be achieved unless the administration and staff themselves have a clear idea of the real needs of their society as a whole, and of their pupils' backgrounds in particular. If the school is to be an effective centre for popular education, it must be in close and continual contact with its surroundings. And even when such contact is achieved, the attitude towards the school as an autonomous institution, the centre of gravity of a world of its own, must be overcome.

Here we are close to the crux of the problem. Asian countries are laying great stress on education. There are still millions of young people who do not have the chance to go to school, and the shortage of teachers and teaching facilities is acute. These days, missing school means missing the basic requirement for life in a modern society; so it is not hard to understand why governments are fighting such a desperate battle to keep up with the increasing population of school-age children. Christian schools play a large part in these national efforts. They cater not only to Christians, but to all creeds and denominations, and their contribution is generally acknowledged and encouraged. Governments entrust schools to Christian organisations; non-Christian parents try and get their children admitted to Christian schools; people join forces to urge the establishment of a Christian school in their area.

At the same time, certain problems arise. Christian schools do not always fit in with national schemes. They retain a high degree of independence and autonomy. Non-Christians begin to ask why it should be that Christian children, having their own schools, thereby also have a better chance of getting an education—and a better education at that—than their own boys and girls.[1] And governments want to know, especially when Christian schools ask for grants or other aid (which they very often get), whether they are going to bow to the national plan, even at the cost of some of their traditional freedom.[2]

The need for state control of education is fairly plain, not only for an equitable distribution of schools throughout the country, but also for a balance of different types of schools in each area. It also provides a safeguard against children being used as guinea-pigs in educational experiments, without any guarantee that their education will be up to the national standards. And so it is reasonable to expect governments to ask private schools to join the national system, especially if a large proportion of the country's children pass through their hands. It is even more important in Asia than in the West that Christians come to terms with their governments in this respect; for the Asian Christian school is an extremely useful centre for the spread of new ideas, and as such

[1] Investigations I made during the "schools crisis" in Ceylon in 1960 disclosed that the Catholic children considered the hostile attitude of the parents of many of their Buddhist fellow students to be due to jealousy—jealousy over the fact that the Catholic schools were the best.

[2] The present policy of the state government of Madras, in India, is to make admittance to all schools free of charge. This appears to be part of a policy of breaking the monopoly of the Christian schools, which will not be able to compete with the government schools.

cannot afford to be isolated from the community, but should be completely at the disposal of all.

Another good reason for Christian schools to examine carefully the implications of their privileged position is that it inevitably arouses the envy of other religions. When another religious group—particularly one that has experienced a considerable revival, and had come to identify itself closely with the native culture—sees the advantages enjoyed by Christian schools and their pupils, it is often tempted to label them as mere agencies for the advancement of Christians in society. In this case, it is useless for the Christians to point out that their privileges were won through their own hard work; for it is quite evident that, in a development that goes on at a national level, it is the duty of the most privileged to do more than anyone else to help the less privileged. And if they will not do this of their own free will, they can expect to suffer handicaps which will enable the others to catch up to their standard.

Any rivalry of this kind between the religions of Asia does considerable harm to the possibility of ecumenical relations in the future. Another feature of Christian schools which disturbs non-Christians is that they often foster what is called a "Christian atmosphere".[1] This is very difficult to define; but it is

[1] This vague term needs a proper definition. Catholics were greatly handicapped during the schools crisis in Ceylon by the fact that, on the one hand, they claimed the right to establish their own schools on the grounds of the need for their children to be educated in a "Catholic atmosphere"; while, on the other hand, they denied that they admitted non-Christian children to those same schools with the purpose or result of having a Christian influence on them.

evident that non-Christian pupils are sometimes submitted to influences which are not in harmony with their life at home.[1] Many non-Christian parents are so grateful to have their children at a Christian school that they turn a blind eye to this. But when they are forced to see the anomaly of the situation, they often become indignant. After all, they reason, because of the high standards of Christian schools, they are practically compelled to send their children there.[2] Is it fair that, in order to get them a good education, they should have to expose them to Christian religious influences? And this approach is perfectly logical; if Christian schools do not want the antagonism to grow, they must take steps to provide the religious education that parents desire. There are instances already in some countries where this solution has been tried. In Pakistan, for example, Muslim pupils now receive instruction in their own religion. But so far there is hardly a single case where it has been done voluntarily by the Christian schools, which implies that the point has not yet struck home.

Christian superiority in education will not last for

[1] Even today it happens that non-Christian children going to Christian schools, especially to the schools of certain Protestant denominations, are compelled to join in prayers and sometimes religious classes. This is especially true of boarding schools, where—for the sake of convenience—Christian and non-Christian pupils are treated alike in regard to attendance at prayers, as in other matters.

[2] It should not surprise us that the same parents who try every means within their power to have their children admitted to Catholic schools, also ask for nationalisation of these schools when the matter comes up for action or discussion.

ever. In fact, its days are already numbered. The extension and modernisation of schools—particularly on the scientific side—is becoming more and more expensive. Technical schools and institutes of domestic science, so badly needed everywhere, place unbearable burdens on a private system.[1] State aid is the only answer; and state aid implies state control. Government schools have to cater to the whole population, and therefore have to set their standards at a reasonable level to begin with, and then gradually to improve them. The standard of Christian schools is bound to drop, especially since the state education is practically free of charge. At present, the high fees that some Christian schools have to ask makes them dependent on the elite who can afford to pay.[2] It is to be hoped that this situation, which will certainly damage the Christian reputation in the long run, will not be allowed to last.

There is one other feature of the Christian educational system which causes some concern. The Christian churches run so many schools in Asia, and

[1] The classic example is Kerala State, which is densely populated and which has the highest percentage of educated people in the whole of India. Christian schools abound, but few of them have facilities for the required level of scientific and technological education. Yet even now the number of such schools is increasing, and no overall planning or coordination seems to be possible.

[2] It would be interesting, if it was not also sad, to note how Christian institutions and groups founded to teach the poor are forced by circumstances to give preference to the children of the rich. And even if the system is used as a means of providing education for the poor, it is often impossible to avoid a degree of visible discrimination.

employ so many people, that they must be considered as business enterprises, despite the fact that they manage to preserve a highly desirable family atmosphere. Sometimes the staff of a Christian school find themselves in a false situation—that is, as both employees, in the normal sense of the word, and co-workers in a non-profit-making organisation. Although they are willing to make certain sacrifices, such as any school demands, they are not willing to forgo the basic rights that any employee expects and deserves. The schools should therefore be very careful to observe normal working conditions, and even to anticipate improvements in rates of pay, hours of work, and so on. The present situation, where many teachers in Christian schools are not even permitted to join their trade union, is bound to alienate the sympathy of the employees, and cause unnecessary conflict.

The teaching staff should also be given more freedom and responsibility in the education of their pupils. This makes their job far more attractive, and offers them a chance to use and develop their creative ability. They should never be treated simply as people who are "devoted" to the school, but must be left free to continue their work outside the school premises; for they are invaluable links with the environment, and can often bridge the gap in cases where a school is not geared to its surroundings. This is particularly true of village teachers. School administrators, who usually come from cities and are better educated than the rural teachers, must avoid imposing their standards on those who are in touch with the common people, and who, however limited their horizons may be, know the local situation thoroughly.

The changes we have suggested here can only be put into effect if the staff-members and the administrators of Christian schools in Asia get together in a spirit of cooperation and make a sincere attempt to set their house in order. It is certainly not a question of their sitting down at a table and discussing academic problems; they must strive to become one body, and to tackle the situation with the widest possible perspectives. True, there is a danger that the status of their own particular school might have to take second place. But if, in return, it becomes a living, vital institution, intimately linked with its environment, and working to keep it growing towards health, then its own identity will be immeasurably enriched.

6

The students

One sometimes hears the youth of Asia described as
a "blind force". This is a most misleading phrase,
and would seem to have been coined by the older
generation as a sign of its feeling of helplessness in
the face of the overwhelming expansion and ever-
increasing energy of the younger population. It is a
false statement of the situation for two reasons: first,
it is discouraging, whereas, in fact, the dynamism of
the young in Asia is far more closely allied to hope
than to despair; secondly, Asian youth is anything
but blind—if it sometimes seems fickle or confused,
because of the rate at which it adopts and discards
ideas, this is rather through having too many eyes
than having none at all. It is not only picking out a
way for itself through the plethora of novelty and
tradition that can be so baffling for the older people;
it is also sighting a line for the whole of Asia to
follow. It would be more accurate to say of the young
that they are the "eyes of Asia".

This means that students—and not only those at
universities and colleges, but those in the higher
grades of schools as well—have a most important
role to play in the development of their countries.
They are among the first to be attracted to modern
ways; they are also at just the right age to be

strongly affected by what they learn. Their position in society should therefore be that of a powerful driving force on the side of progress. If, however, they are not supported by those whose job it is to educate and guide them, they can react in two ways: either they give up their ideals, and settle into a routine job, thus accepting the social system as it stands; or they lose patience with their elders, and support revolutionary ideologies that aim to overthrow even possibly useful features of the old regime, and start again from scratch. It is thus vitally important that teachers and leaders of the student population do not lose contact with the young people who pass through their hands; for schools and universities offer a unique opportunity to gauge—and, to a certain extent, control—the tempo of the younger generation. Once this stage of a person's career is over, he takes his place in society with the rest, and it is far more difficult to evaluate his effect. In secondary and tertiary educational institutions, however, much of the energy and originality of a country is gathered together in such a way that current aims and ideals can be observed, and the results applied in dealing with the students who follow. In this light, education is seen as a two-way process, with those who teach learning just as much from their students as their students learn from them.

Naturally enough, it is not easy to keep in touch with such a volatile group as the Asian student body. There is no ready-made system of neatly arranged "universal" values that could possibly work in a continent as varied and paradoxical as Asia, which, in its present state, is the last place on earth for preconceived methods and ideas. The only feasible approach to education in Asia is to start in the schools and use every conceivable method to teach children—above all else—a sense of responsibility. Not responsibility to the school, which is a dead end; but responsibility to people—to the people in the children's vicinity first, and then, in widening circles, to the whole of their society. This is a self-perpetuating process; for responsibility implies love and enthusiasm, which are highly contagious qualities. It also implies freedom—the freedom to make decisions, and to answer for their consequences. University students already have a lot of freedom of this kind; why not students at school, once they have reached the age of reason? Asian children, particularly in the villages, expect to assume responsibilities far heavier than those of the average Western child, at an incredibly early age. Using this as an advantage, schoolteachers and youth leaders should be able to find ways to build on it, by gradually strengthening the initiative of the children, until they feel they can treat their "masters"—the very word sums up the old approach—more as friends and partners than as directors. This entails, of course, a correspondingly gradual abdication on the part of the teachers, who must finally renounce their own power and influence, in favour of their students, if the result of their labour is to be a creative and responsible generation.

This kind of cooperation can be achieved within the normal pattern of school activities; but if it is to have its full effect, and direct the attention of the pupils to further possibilities outside the school itself, a wide range of extra-curricular activities is an absolute necessity. Such organisations as the Red Cross and the Work Camps movement, youth groups like the Boy Scouts or the Young Christian Students, as well as various other societies that encourage slum work, hospital visiting, and social welfare work in general, not only supplement the training which children receive in school—they are indispensable, particularly in Asia, where they serve as links between the school and the world around it. This is a for more subtle kind of education than the traditionally bookish and school-centred one that has been used up till now; but it is one which is really worth the name. No amount of understaffing or over-crowding can excuse schools from doing their utmost to get some sort of extra-curricular activities under way. It may seem a luxury to appoint special staff-members to look after this aspect of the children's education; but a little reflection will make it clear that such a step is no less essential than the building of libraries and laboratories.

Happily, many schools have already incorporated a certain amount of outside work in their syllabuses. Some have proved successful; some not. The commonest cause of failure is the refusal of teachers to abandon their paternal attitude towards their students. They use the new type of education as yet another means of tightening their control, or increasing the efficiency of the group, or moulding certain pupils into their own idea of what makes a good human being. This negates the whole issue; the students exhaust themselves in activities which *seem* to be theirs, while, in fact, they are simply projections of their teachers' initiative.

Christian schools are no exception in this respect. Children are often organised into extra-curricular activities as an extension of their religious instruction. Since their faith is usually still immature, they sometimes have little or no understanding of what they are doing, or why. Here again, it is a question of gradually initiating them into full responsibility by showing them—through discussion and practical demonstration—that pious actions are not just "good" and "nice" and "Christian"; they are basically social, outward-looking, and practical ways of alleviating needless suffering, and contributing to the welfare of the environment.

Extra-curricular activities are one of the best means of countering the tendency—particularly among students at universities—to feel that their position entitles them to a life of easy work and automatic authority. The idea of a leisured class, safely ensconced in its cliques, paternally condescending to give orders or advice, is inherent in the traditional education system. There is no room for such a facile attitude in modern Asia. It must be replaced by an equally strong tradition of cooperation and social awareness. This will have to start in the schools. Why not in the Christian schools first? The opportunity is there; most Christian schools admit non-Christians, and are surrounded by an overwhelming majority of adherents to other creeds. They therefore provide a perfect place to encourage cooperation and mutual appreciation between the young, which is bound to be continued and developed in the universities and throughout society.

Inversely, it is at the universities that the effectiveness of the schools can be judged. One is immediately struck by the high percentage of university students who are Christian-educated, indicating that there is nothing much wrong with the academic standards of Christian schools. The fact that they are there, however, does not necessarily mean that they are active, nor that they—and more particularly the Christians among them—play the leading role that could be expected of them. Before making any criticism of this group alone, let us consider the general situation of Asian university students.

Apathy is never far below the surface. Many students are short of money, live in dingy lodgings, and have no idea of what they will do when their course is over. They tend to look on the university as a "shop", a place where they do a few years' book-learning to earn a degree or diploma. Apart from their next examination, few things can provoke them to work. All they want to do is finish their studies and start some sort of job, however dull and insignificant it may be. Few groups have the power to organise them, and even fewer leaders can inspire them to action. The foreign nature of many of the student associations available often discourages them, as does the feeling that the previous generation of students were better off, and had more prestige in society than they. Add to this the fact that the teaching they receive is largely academic and divorced from real life, while the example and guidance they expect from their teachers is rarely of a helpful or stimulating nature, and the gloomy picture is complete. It can be summed up by saying that Asian universities run the risk of producing a generation of graduates whose ambition is to get the maximum amount of leisure that a minimum amount of study can procure.

When we consider the enormous handicaps of

Asian students, however, we can afford to be a little less critical. Some might even go so far as to suggest that Asians cut no worse a figure, on the whole, than students in Western universities. For one thing, they are certainly more interested in politics than their Western counterparts, and it is when some emergency situation stirs them to organised action that they show themselves at their full strength.[1] Yet this still does not prove that they are genuinely committed to the cause of social justice; their sense of responsibility towards the underprivileged is often directed little further than their own persons, and many become quite bourgeois and reactionary once they have the security of a job. The irony is that Asian graduates have a far more important role to play in society, relatively speaking, than graduates in the West, who usually have to start their professional life at the bottom of the scale. It is, therefore, essential that the schools and universities realise that the present state of their education system is to blame for the poor morale of students in Asia, and that it is up to them to make necessary changes in attitudes and methods, with a view to injecting some vitality into the jaded student body.

Christians are perhaps more active than most at the university. One thing they have learnt at school is how to organise themselves into societies; Christian student groups offer a variety of services—some spiritual, some material—both to their own kind, and to students in general. They are usually characterised by a spirit of solidarity, and freshmen,

[1] Recent disturbances in Indian universities show how easily an overdose of tension finds an outlet in destructive action.

particularly, find them extremely useful as an introduction to university life. Yet this very spirit tends to cut them off from other religious and social groups, so that they often express themselves in ways which others can interpret as "pressure-group" tactics, or "power-politics" in student affairs.[1] This is not the most effective way of having a Christian influence, since "tactics" of any kind—with all that the word implies—only arouse enmity, and Christian "politics" can cause most awkward complications if Christianity is identified with any particular party, or sets itself up as an independent line. Christians must first establish contact, in a cooperative spirit, with all the other groups who claim to be working for the good of mankind. Only in the light of this broader unity will an ecumenical union of the Christian denominations themselves have any meaning. Asia, which is basically a more friendly place than industrial, war-scarred Europe, could lead the world by achieving even a minimum of this kind of cooperation, and showing its constructive potential at work in society. If anyone should start the ball rolling, it is the students; if any students should be the first to start, it is the Christians.

[1] It is noticeable that action by Christians often follows the pattern of making a stand on so-called "Christian principles", and particularly in a defensive manner— for example, by attacks on Communism or artificial birth control, or by "morality drives".

7

The workers

Asian students are not the only members of their society who want jobs. The vast majority of school-children still have no hope of acquiring more than a basic education, and so will grow up to be workers. That is to say, they will work with their hands—if they manage to get work at all—in jobs that bear little resemblance to the kind their education might have led them to expect. For everyone learns in school that being educated is more or less the key to an easy life. The illusion is eventually broken when they realise that, without a further course in a university or technical college, they simply have no chance of learning the skills and techniques that could lift them out of the manual working-class. If Asia were well equiped with schools that taught trades, it would be a different matter. If there were not such an enormous number of young people demanding an education, and the right to work in a job that suits them, it would also be different. But this is the situation that exists, and the young workers, baffled, perhaps, or frustrated by what seems to them an injustice, fall back on the tools they were born with—their hands.

Their prospects, as things stand, are not bright. Many of them will probably be little better off than their ancestors have been for centuries. They could even be worse off; for the comfort of the traditional inertia they return to will always be disturbed by the knowledge that, with a bit of luck, they could have done so much better. In the past, they might have tried their hand at business, as many Indians and Chinese did, and succeeded. But in those days there was more of a middle-class, and competition was not as strong as today. Now, they are stuck at the bottom of the social scale, and most of their energy is wasted.

The problem, then, that faces every Asian government is how to give these young people a part to play in the development of their country. The workers are certainly not ignorant of the changes taking place. It is in the urban centres that are rapidly growing up around the new Asian industries that a large section of the working population—most of them young—is now to be found, and the workers, through political interest and trade-union activities, keep in fairly close contact with the rate of modernisation. In the rural areas, too, where the great majority of the people still live, radio, and—increasingly—television, offer the world news to even the poorest landless and jobless worker in the country.

Schemes have been proposed for the betterment of the Asian working-class. Educational reforms and programmes for building more technical schools will do something towards solving the problems of the next generation, while movements that aim to teach the dignity and utility of labour have already had a certain effect on the present situation. (The Young Christian Workers organisation is perhaps the best example of a Christian contribution to this effort.)

But these measures are far too slight and slow to be adequate. Striking evidence of what can be achieved by a revolutionary working-class is provided by the successes of the Marxist countries. The minority of workers who are really active, and aware of their people's suffering, are strongly attracted, therefore, to revolutionary philosophies that preach the unity of the world's workers and the establishment of a "workers' paradise". This swing to the extreme Left is one of the most important features of modern Asia, and its effects have been felt in no uncertain way in the West. It cannot help but result in drastic changes in the present feudal and paternal attitude to the Asian worker.

It should be noted here that any progressive movement directed towards the benefit of the working-class is always keen to enlist the support of the white-collar workers. In the West, this group is not really a part of the working-class at all; but, in Asia, where the unskilled, semi-educated "lucky" ones who manage to get jobs in offices as clerks could not possibly—because of their poverty and low living standards—be included in any other social classification, they are considered to be on the upper fringe of the proletariat. This intermediary group wavers between conservatism (if there is a chance of joining the privileged) and revolution (if there is none). It thus constitutes a risky, but potentially powerful and adaptable, set of working-class leaders, since the workers not only appreciate the relative prestige of the white-collar men, but also know them to be of the same class.

On the whole, then, the working-class is in a state of flux. Those who have jobs are often exploited;

they work long hours, and get precious little pay. Because there are so many people anxious to get work, employers have a lot of power; a sudden decision here, or a market fluctuation there, and the workers often suffer as a result. Added to this, there is growing conflict among the workers themselves, which takes the form of a split between generations. The older generation, experienced in their traditional field of work, but not adapted to the technical changes of the modern world, look on the young as a force to be feared. The old hierarchical system of apprenticeship, which included respect for age on the part of the young, and a lot of benevolent paternalism on the part of the old, is unacceptable to the modern generation. Nowadays an energetic young man can, with luck and hard work, be given the chance of acquiring a new technique. In the city, it might be a machine he learns to use; in the country, a tractor. The older workers are far less likely to manage them, or even to want to do it. So the young man finds himself immediately on the same or a higher level than his "seniors". He will naturally demand that he be treated as a fully fledged worker, and his demand will, just as naturally, be met with opposition. But, in the long run, the modern style of labour relations will change the old system, despite the efforts of reactionaries to preserve it, and this will happen even in quite remote rural areas.[1] Sooner or later, all the Asian workers will be affected in some way. If it is to be a peaceful process, and not arouse

[1] The introduction of outboard motors, for instance, into a number of fishing villages in Asia is already causing radical changes in the traditional organisation of an important primary industry.

violent revolution (as it did more than once in the West), it must be thoroughly understood as a necessary and inevitable stage of development, and carefully guided by sympathetic, wise, and patient leaders.

At the moment, therefore, the Asian working-class is, from one point of view, aware of change, conscious of the need for solidarity, and open to influence. Looked at in another way, it is weighted down by a heavy load of traditional conservatism. The net result of these contradictory aspects is insecurity; the workers are like a gently smouldering volcano. What is the attitude of Christians in Asia to these signs of nascent energy in the class that makes up the great bulk of the Asian population?

The first answer that comes to mind is that, on the whole, Christians—especially the clergy and those in leading positions—have hardly even noticed that anything is amiss, despite the fact that peasants and working-class people, who have responded best to Christianity over the years, make up a large proportion of the Asian Christians. The missions have rightly devoted a lot of their time to the under-privileged; working through the traditional Christian organisations, they have managed to build up quite strong and closely knit communities. But times have changed; the kind of unity current among Christians —perhaps adequate in the old days—will not do now. It is too superficial and self-centred to be of much use in anything but a static society. Often it was achieved by leaving the traditional Asian social distinctions untouched; there are many churches in Asia where the congregation is seated according to class, even to caste.[1] With this basis for operation, most Christian leaders thought they were doing enough for the workers by providing religious ceremonies, prayer meetings, a calendar of festivals, and the like, as well as certain social and economic services for the welfare of the people. The rich members of the communities contributed generously to these efforts, and thereby added to their prestige.[2] Admittedly, an enormous amount of good work was done, particularly in the field of education; but the time has now come for a reassessment of the old methods, and a much broader attitude to the problems of the working-class.

For young Christian workers are already disturbing the traditional community life. Many of them are deeply affected by the new features of the labour situation; they see it as a challenge, and they have a lot of questions to ask. At present, these questions are rarely answered within their own Christian community. Because of the ignorance or lack of imagina-

---

[1] In India, and even in Ceylon (where Buddhism has watered down the caste system), separate churches were built for special castes. In urbanised areas pews are being placed in the churches by well-to-do parishioners who claim an exclusive right to occupy them—with the result that, in Negombo (Ceylon), the fishermen threw all the pews into the sea, while in a suburb of Colombo a well-to-do "pillar of the church" petitioned his archbishop to transfer a priest who wanted to make the pews available to all members of the congregation.

[2] There are innumerable "memorials"—in the form of hospital wards, schools, and churches—financed by rich benefactors, sometimes non-Christians at that, which are intended to perpetuate the memory of these donors' generosity.

tion of their leaders, they are forced to pursue their quest outside—a course which is often looked on by those responsible for the maintenance of the tight organisation of the community as disastrous, a betrayal, a form of disintegration, or even of de-Christianisation. Because they consider their Christian groups as "the body of the faithful", distinct from "the world", they cannot conceive of their members joining forces with "competing" organisations, such as socialist political parties or trade unions, even if these cover ground that has not yet been touched.

As a result, they often react by trying to draw the workers back into the safe Christian circle; they intensify religious activities; they expand and reorganise the Christian institutions and social services; and, as a last resort, they ban any kind of allegiance to programmes that do not fall within the traditional limitations of "Christian" theory and practice. In cases where they see that they must accept some new development as inevitable, they arrange a pseudo-social organisation, led—or closely supervised—by the clergy, in order to include it, with as little trouble as possible, within the established system. A perfect example of this process is the organisation of recreation and entertainment for a working-class that has only recently become conscious of the idea of leisure (in the Western sense of the word). A lot of money and energy is spent on such things as clubs, youth centres, and rallies, which attract large numbers of young people. Although these measures are fairly insignificant in comparison with the profound changes that are needed, they often appear to be successful, and so encourage the attitude that anyone who avoids or criticises them is in some way suspect.

All things considered, it is perhaps just as well that the Christian communities have not, on the whole, attempted to create their own labour organisations. Their lack of awareness of the Asian social climate could be a blessing in disguise, for the addition of special departments to deal with Christian workers' problems would only have had the effect of isolating them still more from the main streams of Asian development. As it is, working-class Christians are free to have an influence on the environment in which they work—and to be influenced by it in return—without feeling they have to represent any particular community. They therefore have a perfect chance to be Christian in the broadest sense, by identifying themselves with the whole of humanity, and working side by side with all kinds of people in a cooperative effort to alleviate the world's ills.

They will not find it easy, however. The worst danger is that they will be unable to avoid a kind of double conscience, due to the difficulty of being, at one and the same time, workers in modern Asia and Christians who feel they must be loyal to the traditions that produced them. Their elders in their own community will discourage them from following new paths; the very language of Asian Christianity will seem inadequate to express the problems they encounter. The whole idea of "mother church", for example, will have to be blasted out of its parochial setting and adapted to include a much bigger area. They will fight against those who would keep them "in the flock" without even knowing exactly what is meant by the term. And eventually, perhaps, they will be recognised as very special people, with the urgent task of bearing witness to Christ in the development of his Kingdom.

There are already some hopeful signs. Groups of young workers, inspired by recent theological and practical developments in the West, have achieved considerable success in training themselves and others for the kind of leadership needed by the Asian working-class. They have had the help of young workers from the West—people who have been strongly influenced by the new approach now becoming apparent in modern Christianity towards the place of the laity in the world, and who have studied the suggestions of enthusiastic advocates for the importance of workers—Cardinal Cardijn, for example—and the methods that have sprung up as a result of experiments such as the worker-priest movement. This adaptation of Christianity to the industrial world is still in its infancy, particularly in Asia, where there is a great shortage of leaders to guide the process. But Asian Christianity, because it is less deeply rooted in the past than its "big brother" in the West, and therefore more free to come to terms with the challenge of the twentieth century, is in a position to play a leading part in making this world of labour as Christ wants it to be.

8

The crucial generation

We have emphasised the small number of educated people available to guide the very vast and very young Asian population through a tortuous, and sometimes chaotic, process of change. This adult generation of leaders has naturally put most of its hope in the education of the young, with a view to producing a larger and better-equipped intelligentsia as quickly as possible. Leaving aside the question of whether or not this education is adequate for the kind of leaders Asia will need in the future, it is clear that the present adult generation is the one that counts today. On its shoulders falls the enormous and immediate responsibility of governing, shaping, and educating the Asian countries through the most crucial period of their whole history. Its task is made a little easier by the fact that the total experience of both the East and the West is at its disposal. Furthermore, a small group can often lead successfully when their country's general atmosphere is one of hope— especially if there is also a strong tradition of respect and obedience towards elders, in which case those in authority are likely to be given a good deal of power.

These advantages, however, are more than matched by the difficulties that have to be faced. The almost impossible feat of keeping up with the rate of change, and absorbing all the innovations that are considered desirable for Asia, is something which has to be achieved in a very short time if the present generation is to be of any use to the next. Meanwhile, large sections of the people, inspired by half-digested theories of revolution, are going to start shouting, not only for new leaders, but for a completely new system. To get an idea of the difficulty of being in a position of power in modern Asia, one has only to study the lives of the great leaders. Look at the maze of conflicting factions and ideals that Nehru had to steer his way through in order to pass on to India the knowledge he had learned in the West. All his success and all his failure was plainly visible on the day of his funeral, when his people completely ignored his request for a non-religious ceremony. Western-educated socialist and agnostic or not, on that day he was a Brahmin, if not a god.

The problems which the blending of East and West raise for the educated leaders are reflected all the way down through society, so that each family in Asia must sooner or later feel their effect. Traditional authority is everywhere being put to the test. Parents make all sorts of sacrifices to get their children educated, only to find that this very education is going to shake the family to its foundations. They tolerate as many of the new ways as they can; they are willing, for example, to send their children to a coeducational school, even if they still hide their daughters as soon as a male visitor enters the house. This they do because they think that once the child-

ren are educated, the whole family will be better off.[1]
But clashes are inevitable; the young want to be
understood and guided by their parents, but often
find nothing except what they consider ignorance.
The parents in their turn often misunderstand their
children, and mistake their insecurity for disobedi-
ence.[2] Thus the normal gap between the generations
widens to an abyss, and two quite different worlds
exist side by side, without much communication
between them.

It is a paradoxical situation; those in positions of
authority must lead the young, yet at the same time
they are being led by the young to make changes in
themselves. They react in different ways to this pressure. The conservatives—those who do their best to
carry out their duties in the old style, as teachers,
officials, landowners, priests, and the like, in villages
and towns all over Asia—might seem at first sight to
be the least adaptable to modern influences, and
therefore of least use to the younger generation. Yet
it is they who have the most to offer in one way—

---

[1] Kerala again provides the clearest example. Hundreds
of Keralese girls are studying—medicine, for the most
part—abroad on scholarships; and hundreds more are
being sent to Western Europe for training and even for
work. It is obvious that the place they take up when
they return home will have far-reaching repercussions
on the position of women, and on the whole pattern of
life bound up with it, in Keralese society and in the
Christian community there.

[2] In the course of a survey we made in 1963 of Catholic student life in Asia, we discovered that there is a wide
gap between many of the students and their parents,
even when the parents are educated—and that the
parents are very seldom aware of this gap.

their wisdom and experience can act as a balancing force, a stabiliser, which will have a sobering influence on the more impulsive and erratic elements of Asia's progress. Curiously enough, the middle-of-the-road types—those who have gone part of the way towards compromising with modern developments—are often more of a hindrance than a help, especially when they consider themselves "modern" enough, and baulk at the prospect of going any further. Nevertheless, they, too, can play the role of a buffer between extremes. The third group, which can really be called progressive, will only be able to have its full effect if it scrupulously avoids any tendency to become an exclusive clique—for, in that case, it would inevitably finish up among the less helpful representatives of conservatism.

The problem of Asian leadership—like so many critical aspects of modern Asia—boils down to a question of education. In the present case, it is adult education that is needed; the adult generation must realise that education does not consist of a few years' study in an institution, but is a continual process—a lifetime's process—not only of acquiring knowledge and techniques, but also of applying them to the changing circumstances in which mankind inevitably lives. If the present generation in Asia does not learn to adapt to the modern world, then it will forfeit its right and its duty to educate the young; for the young will change, even if they are retarded by their elders for a time. If the change is to be a cooperative effort between the generations—and anything else could easily be disastrous—the onus is on the adults to make the first move by organising a vast system of adult education under the direction of some of the best brains in Asia.

While we are on the subject of Asian education, we are almost automatically on the subject of Asian Christianity. What is the position of Christians regarding adult education? Can they make a significant contribution? The answer, at first sight, must be: "No"; for Christian adults in Asia need further education even more urgently than other religious and social groups. And one of the most astonishing features of this need is that it is partly caused by the very commitment of Christians to education. Along with a natural pride in the achievements of Christian schools goes a deep-seated idea that school education automatically produces leaders who are suited to the demands of the age. This illusion must be destroyed. Yet how can we expect those who are responsible for Christian education, who for years have been concentrating on the training of the young in their schools—and who have a great sentimental attachment to a system which has cost so much toil and produced such fine results—to turn around and reassess their potential, with a view to the introduction of an adult education scheme and the training of special teachers for this purpose? It would mean a revolution of traditional attitudes. Yet it takes a revolution to catch up with a revolution; Christian educators—from those at the top to the most recently trained village schoolteacher—must see that their own education is at least as important as that of their pupils.

There are many Christian leaders in Asia who are already in contact with adults as part of their work. The clergy of every Christian denomination, for example, are in a particularly good position to be influential. In practice, however, because many of them are traditionally inclined to play the role of the authoritative father of their flock, they have succeeded in alienating many young people—often just the ones who would make the best leaders of progressive Christian movements—and so end up with little more than a nucleus of active but docile parishioners—most of them women—which acts as a barrier to the free exchange of ideas within the community. What changes are made, therefore, occur outside; or, if the clergy do take part, they tend to dictate the limits within which progress is to move. There are also cases of extremely useful reforms, led by the clergy, which never get out of the closed Christian circle into society at large.

The religious leaders, then, need to evolve with the times just as much as the leaders of education. This will obviously be a painful experience; the very idea of adult education for the clergy sounds like an insult. Yet they should be the first to agree that it is essential; if the need for it is made plain to them tactfully, the fact that they are almost without exception sincerely concerned for the welfare of their people—why else would they be what they are? —should be enough to set the process in motion.

What is really retarding the development of adult education in Asia is the ignorance of the urgent need for it. Once this is clear, the rest will follow.[1] It can-

[1] At an informal consultation between the lay people's department of the World Council of Churches and the Catholic laity secretariat in Rome in September 1965, a resolution was passed calling on all the Christian churches involved to give priority to the training of lay

not be too difficult to obtain literature, specialists, and advice from those organisations which have been patiently gathering knowledge and experience in this field for some time now. There will probably be some wastage to begin with, and too much energy spent on projects of limited scope; but eventually systems will be evolved to suit the Asian situation.[1]

One of the long-term effects of this work could be that the laity will at last be given the responsibility they deserve. They, after all, are the parents, teachers, group leaders, trade unionists, politicians, administrators, executives, businessmen, managers, and organisers of the contemporary generation. Their influence can be very great—if they are taught to see the modern world in the light of the gospel, and to

---

people to participate in deciding the churches' financial programmes and even strategy.

[1] As far as Catholics are concerned, a number of meetings have been held in Asia which demonstrate the eagerness of bishops and clergy to catch up with recent developments. In August 1965 there was a meeting in Hong Kong of priests committed to social action in more than a hundred dioceses of the far east and southeast Asia—they came together to study their task in the face of the social problems of this huge area. At almost the same time there was a meeting in Manila of the Asian national student chaplains, organised by the Asian Secretariat of *Pax Romana* (IMCS). Moreover, promising results have been obtained from the re-education of nuns—provided, at least, that the whole congregation is involved in the training programme. Finally, it would seem that the most effective way of achieving continuing education for Christian leaders is by the setting up of mixed teams of adults, comprising laymen of different professions and priests, and covering a particular area.

understand the relationship between God's work and man's with special reference to the particular circumstances of their own country.

Equipped with this knowledge, a re-educated laity could be given far more independence for clerical control, and left free to work in cooperation with their Christian and non-Christian fellows for the good of Asia.

9

The educated laity

There is always a temptation to talk about "adapting" Christianity to Asia. This is misleading, for two reasons: first, it implies that the central message of the gospel can vary from place to place, whereas, in effect, it is only the setting of the message—the language, rites, and traditions used to express it—which can and must change to suit the culture and the period into which it is introduced; and secondly, it inevitably suggests that the adaptation is carried out by a certain group of Christians—the clergy, say, or the theologians—and that "the faithful" merely follow the paths laid down for them.

A far more profound attitude is that Christianity must be *incarnated* into Asia—and the world—in the same way as God himself became incarnate in the man Christ. The recent rediscovery of this essentially Christian doctrine will, sooner or later, have a revolutionary effect on Christian communities everywhere. If Christianity is a continuation of the incarnation of Christ, then every single Christian in the world, because he is a member of Christ's body, has a vital part to play in the humanisation of his environment. The importance of this fact to the laity —traditionally an underestimated force—is inestimable.

We have already pointed out that the tendency of the clergy to extend their basic role as spiritual pastors of their flock—extending it, that is, so that it becomes a paternal kind of domination in affairs which are essentially secular—stems from feudal times, when society was far more static and hierarchical than it is today. The advent of the age of technology has shattered many of the old social categories, and thrown all the emphasis on the basic equality of human beings. Man's aim today is to develop everything the world has to offer, so that everyone can be free from dehumanising injustices. The old mistrust of "the world", which was partly due to common-sense knowledge of its power to corrupt, but which also arose from man's comparative helplessness to control it, has changed to a realisation that it must be mastered by man himself. This is to be the job of the Christian laity, since they are the ones who are most closely connected with it in their everyday work. It is their vocation to handle and organise things—as carpenters, architects, truck-drivers, manufacturers, sculptors, farmers, and so on—in such a way that God's plan for mankind can be fulfilled.

Once we accept the fact that it is the laity who must lead the way in Asia's modern development, it becomes obvious that the educated laymen—for they are in a position to influence and guide their people in the most direct way—stand out as the most important Christian group in society. The extent to which Christianity is successful in Asia is largely dependent on them. They are responsible—more than any other group—for making Christ feel at home in his Asian environment.

There are three guiding principles which they will have to keep in mind if they are to be fully effective, both as Christians and as Asians. The first is that they must be proficient in their job. Educated professional men in Asia may treat their work in a rather disinterested way.[1] This is a kind of betrayal; for, in Asian societies, each profession is accorded a distinct social status, depending on its importance to the well-being of the people as a whole. With this status goes a corresponding prestige, so that unless those who enjoy these professional privileges are fully qualified and profoundly committed, not only to performing their duties, but also to developing their skills to the point of perfection, they are perpetrating a sort of fraud. Those they serve see through the deception sooner or later, and the result is inevitably the disintegration of a valid and sincere social feature, which is at the same time thoroughly Asian.

Secondly, they must be conscious of the tendencies at work in their society. This is a cultural responsibility; they must understand what is native to Asia, and what is new. Above all, they must be able to judge which particular strains can be valuably blended together in their own lives. In this way they can recognise their place both in the development of their country and in the Christianisation of their society. Naturally, it is extremely difficult for one person to combine in himself a profound knowledge of both Eastern and Western cultures. They are not expected to be perfect all-rounders or universal

[1] It is a well-known fact that educated Christians—and perhaps Christian educators—in Asia show little interest in academic careers.

geniuses. But they should at least be adaptable,[1] which means the ability to judge a complex situation, the experience to be able to cooperate in various different projects, the patience to tolerate contradictions, and—above all—a personality broad enough to appreciate many kinds of people. This personal approach to their work, which should be neither static nor unstable, must form the basis of their professional commitment. If each one of them could offer a unique contribution to his society, and at the same time cooperate with his fellows in order to fill the gaps in his knowledge, the result would necessarily be very valuable in the creation of an original Asian culture. For Asia is famous for her diversity, and the new Asian must not sacrifice variety for uniformity. Christians can help her to achieve the kind of unity which they know to exist in the Holy Trinity—three distinct Persons in one Nature. Did not Christ pray "that they may all be one, even as thou art, Father, in me, and I in thee" (John 17: 21)?

The third principle applies equally well to the laity and the clergy. Every educated Christian in Asia must have an *organic* knowledge of his religion. It is not enough to have learnt it from a textbook. Nothing is more of a hindrance to a man than the burden of a static, uncoordinated, and undigested set

[1] The effects of training Asian Catholic priests from their boyhood on have not been encouraging. Those who have gone through this system show little adaptability, and less creativity; and since they look and wait for work to be done by fully qualified people, they often block development.

of rules and doctrines.[1] For a Christian particularly, this kills what should be a living and growing organism. Everyone must realise that there is no easy way of being a Christian. For Asian Christians, this means there is no one style of Christianity that can be bought "off the peg" and put on immediately. Every Christian in Asia is Christianity's tailor. The thought is a little frightening; never before—or, at least, not since the very early days of the Christian religion—has such a small group of people had to carry such an immense intellectual responsibility in their apostolate.

What are the chances that the educated Asian laity will be able to follow these guiding principles, and so have their full effect in society? Their education is already an advantage, for, whatever its inadequacies, it will have given them an opportunity to learn many of the most important technical, philosophical, and social ideas imported from the West. If it has also taught them to observe and compare everything they see around them, then they should certainly have a good start in the arduous process of assessing their respective roles as intermediaries in their country's renovation. Many of them are already intimately involved in the (sometimes violent) debates that arise in Asia whenever the question of design or style is raised. If a new cathedral is to be built in Japan, for example, there will almost certainly be lengthy discussions over whether the style should be traditional Japanese,

[1] This is one of the reasons for the great amount of formalism found among Christian groups in Asia. Sometimes one gets the impression that old superstitions have simply been replaced by new ones.

modern Western, or modern Japanese, or something in between. Christian laymen often support the progressive side in these cases.[1] If they could do as much in every branch of their activities—and know exactly why they chose what they did—they would be helping their country's development in no uncertain manner.

On the other hand, they must cope with formidable disadvantages. One is the tendency among educated Christians to think of everyone else as more or less uneducated. This is an inherited attitude, and arises out of the old "Christian" attitude in the West that the "pagans" were underdeveloped, and therefore primitive, and had to be helped. It also has a lot to do with the deep-seated feudal features of modern Asia, reinforced by colonialism, which make the educated feel they are entitled to power. For the revolution caused by education in Asia has by no means completely replaced the old ruling-class. The children of those in power were the first to make use of modern educational facilities, so that, despite the great increase in the number of graduates, the traditional balance of power is much the same.

This is certainly the main reason why so many educated Christians are no better than the rest of

[1] There is a growing openness among Christian laymen in Asia about this kind of problem. But it would seem that these laymen do not find sufficient response to their own questions and suggestions among other members of their own groups. It is very easy to make contact with people of this kind, and to follow up lines of contact from one person to another; but there is a lack of the coordination which would tap this latent energy and break through the sense of isolation which at present can sometimes lead to frustration and tension.

84

their class. They do their professional work, without feeling obliged to go further and take on "unnecessary" responsibilities. They imagine that, since everyone else is now more or less free to get an education, it is only a matter of time before the most talented of the younger generation come up and join them at the top.[1] Their confidence in institutions and bureaucracy is such that they feel excused from any personal commitment to the task of making sure that this "education", in which they put such faith, is something more than a piece of paper saying that so-and-so is "qualified".[2] And when they do make an effort to play a more positive part—such as taking a leading position in the trade-union movement—they often merely work to strengthen their own hand. There are instances of Asian trade unions, run by educated people, which are used for the political

[1] Even within the relatively small group of graduates the older generation finds it difficult to allow sufficient scope for the ideas and activities of the younger generation. This sometimes leads to a split in graduate organisations, or to the younger graduates withdrawing from them. Sometimes separate graduate organisations have to be set up for the two generations, simply to avoid clashes and to draw out the greatest possible energy and commitment from both.

[2] During the 1963 IMCS (*Pax Romana*) survey in Asia we also contacted graduates in the various countries. We found that more than a few of the graduate organisations did not know what to do or which problems to tackle. Vietnam provides a typical example of the graduate's isolation: though he possesses the necessary education and skill to analyse the situation, he lacks the contact with the people—even with his own Christian people—and the social skill which are required for leadership.

motives of their leaders. Such an attitude proves that these men have little idea of how to make an institution really work for the benefit of the uneducated and underprivileged. The gap between them and the people widens, and remarks like: "The masses are passive", or "The young do not respond", become more and more common. These glib comments are on a par with the old favourites of upper-classes all through history: "What a simple, happy life the ordinary people lead", and, "How quiet and peaceful the countryside is."

Christian intellectuals must divorce themselves from the idea that, because they are Christian, they automatically have more than their fair share of discernment. This is only another aspect of the kind of superiority complex described above. Christian principles—whatever success they might have had elsewhere—still need to be translated into Asian terms. What is even more important, they are not the exclusive property of Christians; nor is there any guarantee that Christians have always understood them, developed them, and practised them more thoroughly than others.

Another problem that will have to be faced by the educated laity is that of their relations with the clergy, and all those whose authority is in the spiritual field. So far, there have been a number of clashes, usually caused by the clergy's interference in lay affairs which do not really concern them. The only way to avoid such misunderstandings in the future, and achieve mature relationships within the Christian communities—along the lines elaborated by modern theology—is for all to cooperate in the basic responsibility which they have in common: that of seeing that the uneducated and underprivileged—Christian and non-Christian alike—are given the chance to lead a full human life. This cooperation would have three distinct advantages: first, it would establish the right atmosphere for a truly Christian collaboration between the laity and the clergy; secondly, it would facilitate the Christian responsibility to communicate with, and come to terms with, non-Christians; and thirdly, it would mean that the educated could fulfil their proper task—that is, to teach people how to teach in their turn.

The combined influence of Christian leaders could therefore be very great. The accent on economic development is so strong in Asia today that people tend to overlook the powerful religious undercurrents which are also a feature of the modern age. The educated Christian laity is a group which spans the whole extent of Asian growth, since it is deeply involved in both the spiritual and material progress of the Asian peoples. If it can make contact with the other sources of these twin energies—both of which are working towards the same ends as the Christians—, then the wisdom and experience of all the Asian creeds can be aligned, and those who love God and want to do his will can work together for one thing he certainly longs to see: the establishment of freedom, justice, and brotherhood among men.

10

The poor

It is evident from the gospel that the poor have a very special place in the kingdom of heaven, and the history of Christianity offers many examples of great men who voluntarily identified themselves with the underprivileged. This does not mean a model Christian is one who is economically poor; despite what Christ said about the rich man's chances of salvation, it does not automatically follow that material poverty is a guarantee of holiness. The usual Christian attitude is that spiritual poverty is the really essential quality for those who would be like Christ, and that material poverty, though not necessary for its own sake, is nevertheless extremely useful, because it is often accompanied by the truly Christian attributes of humility, simplicity, and unsophisticated wisdom. Needless to say, we are not speaking here of destitution; extreme poverty is always pernicious, because it produces want, and has precisely the opposite effect on human beings to that brought about by the Christian ideal, which is, basically, that a man should be satisfied with those possessions needed to make his life—and the lives of his dependents and friends—fertile in all respects.

One of the best ways, therefore, to gauge the depth of Christianity in any particular community is to examine the position of the poor. In Asia, where most people get along on very little, and where many are completely destitute, Christians are put to the test in no uncertain manner, especially since the bulk of the Christian population itself must be ranked with the poorer classes. Let us see how the challenge has been met.

There are two attitudes to the underprivileged, which more or less correspond to the two different connotations of words like "charity" and "sympathy". The true meaning of these terms implies an identification between the doer and the receiver of an action, in which case "charity" is equivalent to "love" and "sympathy" to "empathy". The derived meaning, however, and the more common, is that the doer separates himself from the receiver, so that "charity" becomes "condescension" and "sympathy" is reduced to "pity". We will find that Christians in Asia have usually—for reasons we have already explained—worked along the lines of the second attitude. Certainly, the first thing one notices about Asian Christianity is its enormous commitment to charitable undertakings. This so obviously represents a good, positive, and altruistic effort to help the underprivileged that its motives are seldom questioned. Yet what of its effect on the poor who have received the charity, and, more particularly, on those who have subsequently become Christians themselves?

There is no doubt that converts from the poorer classes have been welcomed into the Christian communities, where they took on a status which they at least consider suitable. All the externals of Christianity were available to them—they could take part in religious services along with their "betters", and the grandeur of the churches made them feel glad to belong. The other buildings—the clergy houses and the various Christian institutions, which were usually the biggest in the area[1] were further proof of the importance of being Christian, and the poor would almost starve themselves to make sure that these solid structures were kept in good order, and new ones erected when necessary.

It would be wrong, however, to give the impression that the foreign standards—and styles—of religious buildings in Asia are simply signs of the Western superiority complex, or that the poor have in any way been exploited. On the contrary, the underlying idea has usually been that nothing could be too good for the faithful, particularly for those who had little besides the faith to keep them going. This is, of course, a basically feudal attitude; and in the past it fitted in well with both the Asian social systems of the time and the deep-seated attitudes of many of the missionaries. Just as, in the European Middle Ages, wealthy noblemen donated the money to construct huge institutions, such as hospitals, orphanages, and

[1] A combination of the Western standard of life imported—and, of course, at least to some degree, inevitably imported—by foreign missionaries, and the special position allotted to clergy in the local Asian situation, has led to the clergy having a different way and style of life. This does not, of course, speak against the real dedication and even heroic sacrifice of many priests; but the fact remains that, as far as the facilities available to them are concerned—training centres, holiday centres, food and drink, transport, nursing services, and so on—the clergy do constitute a really privileged class.

schools—not to mention all the magnificent churches —largely for the benefit of the underprivileged, so, in Asia, rich members of the Christian community were only too happy to give large sums, both for their own prestige, and for the welfare of the people. The paternalistic attitude of the privileged class towards their social inferiors was thereby increased, and the poor accepted it with gratitude.

We should not condemn previous generations for an approach which was, after all, in keeping with the times. But nor should we for one moment imagine that the situation they established should be allowed to continue in modern Asia. The current Asian social changes, even before they are exploited by extremists as a weapon against the ruling-class, are tending more and more to alienate the sympathy of the lower classes from those they have traditionally revered for centuries.[1] Many already regard Christianity with suspicion, or even hatred, and underprivileged Christians who have not only benefited from Christian social services, but once identified themselves with the whole system, now speak of the church as "rich".[2]

[1] In the countryside district of Ceylon where I worked for a number of years, Catholics called their priests "chicken-eaters". There was not necessarily any bitterness or malevolence in this—indeed, the custom showed something of that real tenderness and affection which led the Catholic people to treat their clergy well. But it is clear that this privileged position of the clergy can one day grow into a serious challenge and cause of tension.

[2] Everywhere in Asia one can hear lower middle-class and poor Catholics complaining that their children are not admitted to Catholic schools, while the children of rich Catholics and non-Catholics alike are admitted

This is a very sad state of affairs indeed, as it shows immediately that they have made a distinction between themselves and those who run the church institutions. If the latter are considered as "the church", then, clearly, the poor regard themselves on its fringe only. As a result, many start looking around for something better. Some are lucky enough to find a Christian group that strives to cut paternalism to a minimum and to encourage the active participation of all its members. In this way, they may even discover "genuine" Christianity. But others prefer to believe those who tell them that "the church" is oppressing them.

It is almost a sociological fact that, when this sort of thing occurs, the greater the former confidence in the old system, the deeper the hatred of it when the tide turns. (The rise of the Italian Communist Party provides a classic European example of this process.) The younger generation in Asia live in two worlds. They are surrounded by inertia on the one hand, and tremendous energy on the other. This makes them extremely changeable, much to the

---

because of the financial support behind them. School administrators openly regret that they are compelled to give in to this unhealthy system. And there is another factor: after being trained in those Western countries which are responsible for various progressive social institutions in the churches, clergy often consider themselves "progressive" on arrival in an Asian country. They may well set themselves up as "keepers of progressiveness", and this is dangerous—for it will make them conservative in many respects at the same time as making it impossible for them to realise the fact. This, I am sure, is often the cause of the dissatisfaction which tends to be found among this group of clergy.

astonishment and chagrin of conservatives. Imagine the reaction of the clergy, for example, when Christian primary-school teachers, who used to be their right-hand men, suddenly show themselves violently anti-clerical! Such quick changes can perplex and sadden even the progressive clergy who have been trying to impart more than a superficial understanding of the Christian way of life, and to establish relations of mutual confidence with their people.[1]

If Christianity is to keep pace with the breakdown of the Asian feudal system its leaders must realise, not so much that the old ways were wrong, but that a changing Asia calls for new ways—new ways that cannot be plucked from the air, but must follow from a thorough examination of all the possible means of making a harmonious transition from one set of circumstances to another. To do this they must understand exactly why Christianity and feudalism, like Christianity and colonialism, went hand-in-hand in the past, and why they must now separate. Otherwise there is a grave danger of Christians finding themselves left behind as conservatives. One has a vivid picture of the clergy preaching the good old days to empty churches—empty, that is, except for the privileged sitting behind their name-plates in the pews they have bought for themselves.

We have spoken mostly of the externals which Christianity offered to the poor. But what sort of teaching were the poor given about their religion? It is interesting to note that, apart from the rather

[1] This applies to Catholics especially, of course. The so-called "sects" suffer least from this particular problem, and constitute a real challenge to the established churches in this respect.

mechanical and sentimental quality of traditional Christian methods of religious education for the unsophisticated, the accent was nearly always more on the Old Testament than on the New (which is far from implying a proper biblical catechesis). That is to say, it was found easier to teach the ten commandments than the eight beatitudes. This moralistic attitude implies a conscious or unconscious belief that a profound understanding of the Christian revelation is beyond the grasp of ordinary people.

Such a pessimistic view has never been officially a part of the doctrine of any of the Christian churches, and would seem to completely contradict the spirit of the gospel. Yet even at the higher educational levels, where the most talented received a great deal of religious instruction, the sort of teaching that was handed out could only be described as "potted theology", which was rarely put into Asian terms, and had little to do with the daily life of the pupils.[1] If this was the case at the top, one can imagine that the instruction given to those who received no religious education besides what they heard from the pulpit,

[1] I once instructed a Chinese student for baptism. One Saturday I explained the eucharist to her, starting from the meal which was organised in her home on the anniversary of her father's death. I met her again on the following Monday. On the intervening Sunday she had heard a sermon at mass on transubstantiation, and she was almost in tears. She would never become a Catholic, she said, because Catholic doctrines were so difficult. And yet, on the previous Saturday, after my explanation, she had been happy because she had for the first time understood something that had always been a mystery to her before.

consisted mainly of sentimental stories, or simplified summaries of what the more privileged were taught.

This system, which is presumably what generations of educators have thought to be the best, and which still continues to be used extensively in Asia, cannot in any way contribute to the making of mature Christians, much less mature communities. The old theory of an educated elite who—the missionaries imagined—really understood the joyful message of the gospel, even if the unsophisticated could not, is a very back-to-front kind of Christianity. For the educated could not possibly understand the gospel unless they saw that it was primarily directed to the poor in spirit, and that they themselves were supposed to be in this category. For the poor—in whatever sense the word is taken—must occupy a very special place at the heart of the Christian community. It is not as an outlet for their "charity" that the educated need the uneducated, but as their brothers in the faith, whom they can certainly serve if they like—but who will probably be of greater service to them, the educated, in the long run, by helping them to understand their religion in a more profound way.[1]

The unsophisticated have a wisdom all their own, and one which is particularly valuable for all Christians. Any community in which they are neglected is

[1] "There is no basis whatever for their impertinent assumption that *they* must accept *you*. The really terrible thing is that *you* must accept *them*. You must accept them and accept them with love. For these innocent people have no other hope. They are, in effect, still trapped in a history which they do not understand; and until they understand it they cannot be released from it." (James Baldwin, *The Fire Next Time*.)

bound to remain immature. This is suddenly becoming very obvious in Asia, since the poor are finding their voice in other ways. Let us hope that the modern attitude of the more progressive elements in the Christian churches continues to work for necessary changes.

We are not suggesting here that the Christian institutions in Asia, which do so much to better the lives of the poor, should be reduced. On the contrary, it could well be that more will be needed. But as long as the institutional approach, which seems to require palatial buildings and heavy financial backing, remains the most obvious and distinctive feature of Christianity in Asia, the churches will be out of touch with the people—people who, because they are most closely connected with the spirit and substance of Asia, are vitally important to the survival and growth of Asian Christianity.

Institutionalism means that many of the most influential Christians are isolated from the underprivileged, and never share their lives in any way. The number of Christian leaders who actually go and live with the people—in the countryside, for example, or in industrial centres—is very small. A few contemplative monasteries and convents have been established in Asia, but their effect has been minimised by their old-fashioned methods. It is perhaps not a bad thing that great agricultural religious communities—like the monasteries of the Middle Ages—did not become the standard basis for the Asian apostolate.[1] For they would only have

[1] For the average Asian Christian, joining one of the existing contemplative monasteries would amount to a stepping-up of his standard of life. There are exceptions,

provided so many more examples of Western-style Christian life. This is not what Asia needs. The accent should be squarely laid on catering for the normal type of "Christian-in-the-world". It would be naïve to imagine that the traditional Christian orders, transplanted to Asia, would have contributed much to the making of mature Christians. They might even have had the effect of prolonging the competitive spirit which has blotted their copybook in the past—and which is certainly not wanted in Asia today, where cooperation is so urgently needed.[2]

On the other hand, a system could be devised whereby some of the Christian organisations that do social and educational work in Asia could devote a certain proportion of their energy to unpretentious projects which would aim to share more intimately in the lives of the people. The most important point to be kept in mind is that any kind of condescension must be scrupulously avoided. It is not a question of being good enough to help the underprivileged; it is simply that the average type of Asian Christian is— precisely—the man in the street, the man behind the plough, the layman in the world. It is not his fault if he needs help; and he will repay what he owes— true charity—in kind, and many times over.

---

of course—but only where a real attempt has been made to create an original and Asian form of the contemplative life.

[2] The place of missionary societies and other similar institutions among the young, local churches is a serious problem today. It is not just a question of cooperation and coordination, but one of money as well—naturally enough, the missionary societies' lines of communication are more efficient than those of the local churches.

11

Towards an Asian Christianity

What we have said so far by no means constitutes an ordered plan of action; it has simply tried to describe a state of affairs which Asian Christians will, sooner or later, have to tackle. We have devoted a good deal of space to an evaluation of the kind of Christianity that Asia has inherited from the West, and the disadvantages of trying to make this kind of Christianity fit countries which are undergoing radical changes in their social organisation. The West can still be of great help. Its universities and research groups include many people—Christian or not—who are deeply interested in Asian problems. The various Christian bodies also have a lot to offer, as long as they refrain from imposing their ideas, which are often not supported by sufficient practical experience. The one thing which must be avoided is the direct imitation by Asian Christians of apparently successful features of Western Christianity. Apart from the fact that the Western churches are in the middle of a far-reaching revision of their own position in the modern world, there is no guarantee that what has worked in the West will work in Asia.

One aspect therefore, of the new approach that

will have to be applied by Asian Christians involves patient and detailed examination of what may be called "Gothic Christianity", with a view to salvaging as much of their inheritance from the West as can be practically applied in their own circumstances. They will probably find—as Christians in Europe and America have been in the process of finding for almost a century—that the Christianity built in the Middle Ages is like a vast and magnificent cathedral which has weathered the storms of history with remarkable success, but is now beginning to crumble under the winds and rain that were never predicted by its architects. When the cost of maintaining such a structure begins to cripple those who pray in it, a compromise must be made. It will be found too high, too rigid, too strongly fortified. Its new architects will therefore design it closer to the ground; its materials will have more give, more elasticity, enabling it to move a little with the worst shocks, and not crack; and, lastly, it will be in harmony with its landscape, so that those who pass by will know it belongs with them, and that they can worship in it without being wrenched out of the everyday world which is familiar to them.

Though the second aspect of the task facing Asian Christians will be even more difficult than the first, it is important that they set about it at the same time lest the first should remain incomplete. It is a question of discovering the character of Asia—or, rather, of each Asian country—in order to see which Asian features can safely be incorporated in a newly designed Asian Christianity. This will be a vast undertaking, since it covers a far broader field than the investigation of Christian history. It will mean approaching the great Asian religions, to gauge which of their traditional doctrines and methods and customs are valid in contemporary Asia, and which seem doomed to destruction by the forces that are at work all over the modern world. Then, and only then, these religious characteristics of Asia—which are also cultural features, given the close bond between culture and religion in Asian history—will have to be re-examined, to find out whether they run counter to the essential spirit of Christianity as written in the gospel, or whether in fact they have something to add and can enrich the lives of Asian Christians.

Let us pause here to consider the example of a feature which is fairly typical of Asian religions, but has hardly even been considered as a potentially vital part of Asian Christianity. We have already mentioned the fact that Christian monasticism never really caught on in Asia. This is a strange omission, considering how keen the missionaries were to introduce so many other features of Christianity as it had developed in the West. Nowadays, of course, many would say it was just as well that the contemplative sort of Christianity was underemphasised, since Asia now needs social workers more than monks, economic development more than methods of meditation, technicians more than philosophers; and they would reinforce their argument by pointing out that even Buddhist monks, among others, are tending more and more to take an active part in such worldly affairs as politics and social welfare work—why, then, should time be wasted on anachronistic experiments like trying to adapt Christian monasticism to Asia?

Be that as it may, the scarcity of Christian monasteries in Asia has had important results. For one thing, although Asian Christians are known to be, on the whole, keen on prayer and the devotional aspects of the Christian life, and although they have been described by both Eastern and Western observers as more contemplative by nature than most Westerners, they seem to know little or nothing about the long history of Western monasticism. The great mystical experience of men like Ruysbroeck, Bonaventure, or Bernard of Clairvaux, and the voluminous writings on meditative aims and techniques that were produced by the medieval monasteries, have hardly penetrated to the Far East.[1] Nor are Asian Christians familiar with the highly developed meditation methods of, for example, Hindu and Buddhist monasticism.

On the other hand—and this is the irony of the situation—the West is becoming increasingly interested in Eastern achievements in this field, and some Christian monasteries have already adopted certain Oriental features into their routine of prayer. Such book titles as *Christian Yoga* and *Zen Catholicism* bear witness to this new attitude. Non-Christians are particularly attracted to Eastern mysticism—especially people who have explicitly rejected Chris-

---

[1] It is a pity that only Western Christianity has made an impact on Asia in mission work. Apart from the great Nestorian apostolic movement, which lasted until the Moslem expansion disrupted its lines of communication, the wealth of Eastern theology and rites has not been at the disposal of Asian Christianity. The small pockets of Eastern Christians on the Malabar coast have always been isolated communities.

tianity, and turned to an alternative path to salvation. There is a lot of obscurantism and false eclecticism mixed up with this, of course; but there is also a lot of genuine appreciation and humble search for the truth—so much so that missionaries are sometimes sent to the West from Asia in answer to the demands of those who are interested in the faith they represent.

It is clear, therefore, that the Christian under-estimation of Asian monastic traditions has resulted in an opportunity being missed of bringing the two halves of the world closer together. Even now—especially now, perhaps, considering the wild pace of modern life—there is a need for contemplatives who can spread their spirituality throughout society, and help people to lead a more balanced existence. We do not for a moment suggest that Asia should suddenly import, or have thrust upon it, the whole range of Western monastic orders. Asian Christians must be completely free to accept or reject anything that has not been thoroughly examined and assessed for its suitability for Asian conditions. Whether they choose from the East or the West is surely of little import-ance. The main thing is to be certain that what is chosen fulfils two conditions: first, that it should harmonise with the local situation; and secondly, that it should be in accordance with the spirit of the gospel, especially with the gospel's emphasis on childlike love and spiritual poverty.

These conditions apply, of course, to all aspects of Asian Christianity. They are deceptively simple, for Asian society is extremely diverse and subtle. But sticking to our example of monasticism, and leaving aside all preconceived ideas about how it would work in practice, we are left with four very general suggestions. First, the living standards of those who "leave everything" to devote themselves to the work of doing God's will should be such that the poor cannot justly ridicule them. If, for instance, the superior of a monastery in Asia has to fly to America every year to raise funds, the Asian poor can be pardoned if they laugh up their sleeves. Secondly, though their lives may reasonably seem a little strange to the local people, they must never under any circumstances seem foreign. Thirdly, a particular style of monastic life should avoid giving the impression that it is the best or only way of achieving spiritual perfection. And fourthly, the distinctive— but not, I hasten to add, ostentatious—feature of any monastic group should be brotherhood.

This example we have chosen to illustrate some of the shortcomings and difficulties in Christianity's effort to become truly Asian can be multiplied many times over. Across the whole range of Christian activity much the same problems occur. The temptation for outsiders—Western theologians, for example, or the heads of Christian international organisations—is always the temptation to theorise about Asia without a deep enough knowledge of Asian conditions. There should be an unbroken chain stretching from them to the Asian people and back through the medium of the Christian leaders in Asia—though the Asian clergy, schoolteachers, labour leaders, and educated laity in general, all of whom have the dual responsibility to inform the planners of the people's needs, and to put into practice the solutions that are then suggested. But in actual fact the chain does not reach as far as the people. We have already done our best to explain why. We have described how the schools tend to be self-centred, how the educated Christians think of themselves as privileged, and how the clergy are sometimes out of touch with all but the most servile members of their flock. If this isolation is not broken down, how can the Christians who really have ideas about possible remedies for the problems of Asian Christianity ever be well enough informed to do their job properly?

The situation is complicated by several further "short-circuits". For one thing, both Asian and Western Christians depend for their information about Christianity in Asia on their own press agencies, mission literature, and special publications. Much of this is misleading. A careful analysis of news reports on some of the most notable instances in which Asian Christians have had their position radically altered by political events shows unmistakable evidence that facts have been edited and presented in a one-sided way.[1] It is necessary for us to turn to the general press if we are to correct certain

[1] During the government of Mr and (especially) Mrs Bandaranaike in Ceylon, the Catholic press all over the world reported on the events which led—among other things—to the nationalisation of mission schools as if a fully fledged persecution was in train. Let me quote a personal instance to make the point: in 1961 we organised a work camp in Ceylon, in which nuns took part for the first time. Photographs were published in the Catholic press. When they saw one of these pictures, some Sinhalese nuns who were at the time being trained in the French mother house of their order burst into tears—they thought that the nuns had been photographed in a concentration camp!

impressions systematically fostered by Christian publications. We can then see that Christian editors have sometimes made what can only be described as "intellectual somersaults", in an effort to make orthodox views fit in with unexpected developments.[1] This is a deplorable state of affairs, more particularly because it represents a closed circle. The news is drawn from Christian sources in Asia, usually edited in foreign countries—and then redistributed among the Asian Christians, thus reinforcing the very ideas that are at the root of many of their worst dilemmas.

Another fault in the "system" is that the theorists are not in close enough contact with Christian leaders who are on the spot. They should travel more in Asia, live there for a while, and get to know the difficulties that have to be faced by Christians in an Asian society. Many of the teachers, missionaries, and laymen in an influential position have creative ideas and sound criticisms to offer. But there is a strong tendency for them to get tired of being misunderstood, and even suspected, by their superiors and their colleagues. Admittedly, some of their suggestions might be somewhat immature; but, equally, others might be brilliant and—whatever the case—it is not a good sign that these people feel ignored, misjudged, or persecuted. The obvious solution is for more cooperation and constructive exchange of ideas

[1] During the regime of President Diem in South Vietnam, the Catholic press portrayed him as an outstanding example of a Christian leader in a country where Christians constitute only a small minority. After his downfall the same press often painted him black, without ever attempting to depict him and his activities in the light of the real Vietnamese situation.

and experiences, not only between them and the planners, but also between the various bodies in Asia which are doing similar work.

A word of warning should be given here: no matter how many reforms are made to this chain of communication between theory and practice, it is essential that the common people—the average Asian Christians—play a part in it proportionate to their importance as the lifeblood of Christianity. Otherwise the present paternal approach will be prolonged, and will do untold damage to the Christian churches in Asia. Not only this—and it is a big enough task, in all conscience—but the cooperation between the various levels of the Christian communities will not be fully effective until it is extended to include the other groups—Christian and non-Christian—who are also at work in the rebuilding of Asia. Let us conclude with a brief look at the possibilities of an "ecumenical" approach along these lines.

12

Asia and ecumenism

The fact that the unity of the Christian church has been shattered into various denominations is one of the greatest obstacles to its progress. Its discordant and competitive divisions are a source of ridicule among non-Christians, and of scandal among Christians themselves, now that recent events in the world have made them more conscious of the need to discuss their differences, and present a common answer to the growing challenge of atheistic humanism. The ecumenical movement is still in its infancy; but it is the most hopeful sign in the Christian church for several centuries.

Asian Christians are particularly aware of the disadvantages involved in having rival churches within the Christian body. This is partly caused by their being in a minority, and therefore in need of all the potential strength of a combined Christian force if they are to have their full effect on a sometimes unsympathetic or even hostile environment. But a more valid reason is the sheer waste—in countries that are desperately short of the basic requirements for development—of having several different Christian organisations doing more or less the same work.

This duplication is most obvious in the Christian education systems, though it applies—in varying degrees—to almost all the other Christian institutions and activities. It is more noticeable in education, simply because education is modern Asia's most vital aspect. Imagine a situation—by no means uncommon, especially in the villages—where two or more schools have been set up by different Christian denominations, and work almost side-by-side to provide roughly the same education. To make it worse, the relations between such schools have often been none too friendly—and even where tolerance prevailed, the independent struggle of each school to attract children, maintain its standards, and look for sources of financial aid often involved it so thoroughly in its own difficulties that it had little opportunity of making ecumenical overtures, or working out a plan for a cooperative effort.

In defence of this arrangement it might be suggested that, since each school was better than any supplied by non-Christian bodies, more children had the opportunity of a good education. Even if this was true once, it is certainly not true today. Leaving aside the question of whether a single cooperative school would have done a better job, and cost less to establish and maintain, the most obvious reason for a combined effort is that it would enable a more varied range of education to be offered. Instead of two schools providing a general education, one would teach trades—or whatever particular kind of curriculum the district most needed. In this way Christians could do a lot to help Asian countries produce enough educated people to meet local demands.[1]

[1] Another reason for considering seriously an integration of the Christian schools systems into the national systems is the fact that, in many Asian countries, the

Another excuse often used to justify the extravagance of denominational schools is the basic right of each Christian group to teach the kind of Christianity it believes. This hackneyed argument will certainly no longer bear close examination. Although, up till now, it might have been a matter of principle for Christian schools to provide, not only a general Christian atmosphere and education, but also a particular training along denominational lines, their right to do is bound to be limited in the near future. Quite a number of schools have already compromised considerably in this respect in order to obtain much-sought-after government grants. They have not only opened their doors to non-Christians—who are often in a majority, even on the staff—, but they have also bowed so respectfully to government conditions that they refrain altogether from teaching religion! The Christian pupils receive instruction in their faith in separate Sunday-schools.

This innovation would seem to invalidate entirely any competition between the denominations. Even if the sacrifice of their traditional freedom is made only under pressure of financial needs or features of national development, they must surely see that there are equally strong moral issues involved—the scandal of Christians competing with each other in the name of Christ, the waste of money and talent, the creation of privileged groups, and so on. On the other hand, if the sacrifice were made voluntarily, in a positive

Christian schools receive a very high proportion of the state grants for private schools. This fact demands a bold and detailed assessment of the service which these Christian schools render to the countries concerned.

attempt to further the cause of Asian education, it should not prove difficult to profit from such idealism, and get the representatives of the various denominations to sit down together and work out—in a spirit of brotherhood—a system that would answer the needs of Asians.

Yet even if this succeeded—even if a spirit of cooperation spread through all the Christian activities, and Asian Christianity presented a united front, it would still not be enough. Western Christians could be tempted to think of "Christian ecumenism" as a kind of total solution! Asians, never. For they know that they are hopelessly outnumbered by the adherents of other religions, and that, in the social and economic development of Asian countries, they will have to use what influence they have as a stimulus or leaven, keeping constantly in mind the right of the majority to decide their destiny. For Asian Christians, therefore, the ecumenical movement covers a lot more ground, its aim must be not only to unite Christians, but to extend this search after unity to all the Asian creeds by going out to meet the non-Christians, starting a sincere dialogue with them, and trying to combine the efforts of all men of goodwill.

In other words, it will be the specific task of Asia to prove to the world that it is impossible to "creep up on God", to become Christian bit by bit, or stage by stage. It must be done all at once. The idea of first uniting Christians and then beginning to approach the other religions is not in the spirit of the gospel. Even if it could be achieved, the kind of Christianity that would result from such a union would be quite out of touch with its non-Christian surroundings. It would almost certainly be closely modelled on the system evolved in the West, which is a product of unique historical circumstances, and far more limited than is generally admitted. For a truly Asian Christianity, the basic approach must be found in the gospel.

This is not to suggest that Asian Christians should abandon their institutions and organisations and return to the forms and methods of early Christianity. But, inspired by the example of the first Christians, they must reform and develop what they have so that it suits modern Asian conditions. Asia undoubtedly needs the kind of institutions and organisations on which the Christians have concentrated; but they could be made far more effective if they came out of their isolation and realised that there will be no room for privileged groups in Asian societies of the future. All the signs point to the fact that Asia will have to socialise to a large extent if she is to manage her growing population. Christians will have to co-operate with governments in their endeavour to provide social justice for all.

But Christians must go further still. They must see that they are not the only religion in Asia that is in the process of revival. More and more adherents of other Asian religions are coming round to the idea that the development of the world for the good of men is in no way contradictory to the tenets of their faith. As this realisation grows the need for coopera-tion will become increasingly evident. Laymen at least will have to put aside their religious differences and work together for the general welfare, while those in positions of religious authority will have to do their utmost to smooth the way for them and give them the spiritual support they need if they are to progress according to God's will for man.

This is surely a most exciting prospect and one which offers Asia a special place in the building of God's kingdom. There are already enterprises under way which give some idea of the pattern of the future. In Djakarta, for example, a Catholic university has been opened, which is run solely by laymen; this is the first of its kind in the world, and it is hoped that, through its efforts, a new type of dialogue will be started.[1] Again, a fine example of willingness to cooperate is provided by an orphanage which has been set up by a neutral organisation in a predominantly Catholic area, with an Anglican woman in charge of a Catholic staff, and with Buddhist, Catholic, and Protestant children all able to receive instruction in their own faiths. And a third example is provided by the Swallows, a Swedish volunteer organisation: in collaboration with Civil Service International, they have initiated a scheme for rehabilitating pavement slum dwellers at Tondiarpet, in the suburbs of Madras. This scheme is fully supported by the municipality, and by the Catholic student organisations (All-India Catholic University Federation). It is to be hoped that such experiments

[1] Yet this university—Atma Jaya—is all too clear an example of the difficulty experienced by lay enterprises seeking financial support abroad. Universities run by religious institutions or by the hierarchy have their network of communication, but lay universities do not. Moreover, by tradition the money collected from lay people goes to the hierarchy or to religious institutions —and these same lay people are now expected to find money over and above what they are already contributing for what is regarded as their "own enterprise".

prosper and multiply, for they show plainly that Christianity is a universal religion—and they also encourage non-Christians to feel confidence in it, and a sense of brotherhood with it, thus facilitating future cooperation.

On the other hand, it is often asserted that the time is not yet ripe for a meeting between Christianity and the other religions. This is hard to believe. Admittedly, there are many obstacles to be overcome, but the fact remains that Christians and non-Christians are already in contact at most social levels. They often coexist in the same family. They work together; they shop, travel, mourn, and rejoice together, rubbing shoulders in dozens of different situations. The leaders of the Christian churches are usually unaware of the extent and importance of this intercourse, so thoroughly has the real position been hidden behind the docility of those who surround the local clergy.

As a result many Christians suffer pangs of conscience because their daily life and the teaching of their religious leaders do not seem to agree. They are broad-minded enough to respect the beliefs of others, and see no reason why they should not attend funerals and feasts organised by members of other religions and denominations, or share their lives in many ways.[1] At the same time they keep this from

[1] A mature Christian teacher once asked me whether the practice which she and a few Catholic friends had carried on when they were at their teachers' training college—they had prepared meals for the Buddhist students who had gone to the Temple for their full-moon ceremony—was right. She wondered what I thought of this gesture, and told me that she had not dared to talk

those in authority over them, fearing that it might clash with the rules and regulations imposed from above. This has a doubly bad effect: it makes them feel guilty, and it prevents open dialogue taking place between the different religions. It is a perfect example of the lack of real communication and understanding between the Christian leaders and the ordinary people of the Christian communities.

Many of the finest Christians in Asia are deeply disturbed by the reluctance of their leaders to discuss the theological problems involved in the meeting of Christians and non-Christians. Those whose sympathies lie with the working-class probably worry most of all about this, since they are up against the practical impossibility of mobilising the workers without the cooperation of the different religions. Until the religious question is brought into the open, and Christian workers feel free to join forces with their non-Christian brothers, progress is inevitably retarded.

The educated Christians—whom one would expect to be the most helpful in this respect—are perhaps the most handicapped. Through their education they have imbibed the cautious and shortsighted attitudes of their leaders towards the non-Christian religions. On the other hand, they have been taught more about Christianity than others, so that there is a good chance that—once the ecumenical process is set in motion—they will quickly adopt a more mature

---

to a priest about it before—she knew that it was in the spirit of the gospel, but at the same time she had always felt that it would have been disapproved of by the clergy.

outlook and play an important part. (Their experience with non-Christians in their school and university life will then be an added advantage.) There is no need to stress here again that adult education is the only way to speed up the participation of the educated in this as in so many other aspects of Asia's progress.

It is good to be able to say that a certain amount of basic research into the possibility of a genuine encounter between the Asian religions has already been carried out, mainly by Protestant Christians.[1] Yet the reactions have been relatively feeble. None of the religious bodies has made any enthusiastic effort to define its character, or to publicise itself, with an ecumenical aim in view. It is surprising that Christianity has not shown much initiative in this respect, considering its achievements in the intellectual field. In one way this is most unfortunate, for it takes a long time to build up a generation of experienced thinkers and teachers who can develop new aspects of theology and also popularise the results of their work. But, in another way, it is a blessing in disguise. For Christianity is much better prepared now for dialogue with other religions. It has matured enormously during this present century; its outlook is more universal, and its contact with the real world more profound than fifty years ago.

[1] This is a suitable point to mention two important contributions by Protestants: Japanese Protestant theologians have already made considerable progress towards elaborating a "Japanese Christian theology", and the Christian Institute for the Study of Religion and Society at Bangalore has published a large amount of valuable literature on religious and social problems in India.

Of all the religions in Asia, it should certainly be the first to make an ecumenical gesture.

The other religions are beginning to break through the boundaries set them by history. Buddhist and Hindu missionaries preach in the West. The obvious result of this encounter between the religions will be a cross-fertilisation of the greatest spiritual forces in the world. At the same time Marxism continues to make strides. Atheistic or not, it must be accepted as a creed. The same principle applies to encounter between Marxism and the religions of the world as to encounter between Christian and non-Christian religions. It is no use uniting one group in order to oppose it to another, if both can possibly be considered to have similar aims. If Christianity manages to come to an ecumenical understanding with the other religions, then it must—and at the same time —open itself to contacts with atheistic creeds with a view to the greatest possible cooperation with them.